W9-BMG-136

Botanica's

100 Best

PERENNIALS

FOR YOUR GARDEN

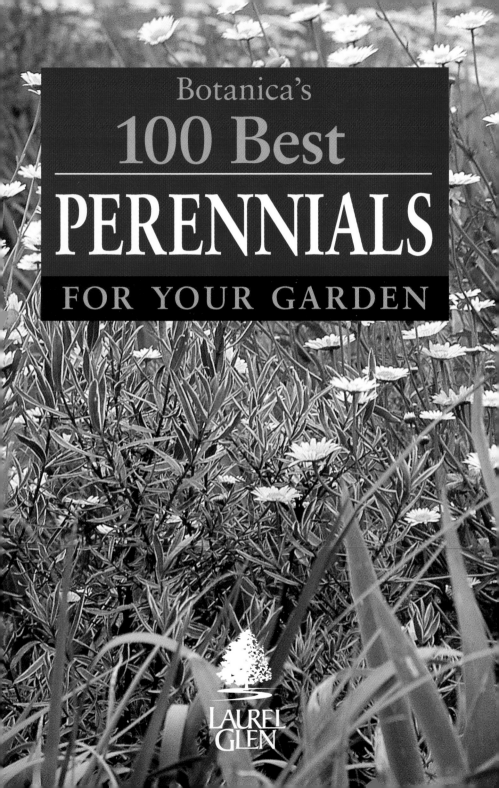

Botanica's
100 Best
PERENNIALS
FOR YOUR GARDEN

LAUREL
GLEN

First published in 2000 in North America by
Laurel Glen Publishing
An imprint of the Advantage Publishers Group
5880 Oberlin Drive, San Diego, CA 92121-4794
www.advantagebooksonline.com

Text © Random House Australia Pty Ltd 2000
Photos © Random House Australia Pty Ltd 2000 from the
Random House Photo Library

All rights reserved. No part of this book may be
reproduced, stored in any retrieval system or transmitted
in any form or by any means, electronic, mechanical,
photocopying, recording or otherwise, without the prior
written permission of the Publisher.

ISBN 1-57145-473-X
Library of Congress Cataloging-in-Publication Data
available upon request.

1 2 3 4 5   00 01 02 03 04

Publisher: **Penny Martin**
Consultants: **Geoff Bryant and Geoffrey Burnie**
Managing editor: **Jane Warren**
Text and picture research: **Susan Page and Karen Winfield**
Design: **Juno Creative Services, Sydney; Bob Mitchell**
Cover design: **James Mills-Hicks**
Page makeup: **Arc Typography, Sydney**
Production manager: **Linda Watchorn**
Film separation: **Pica Colour Separation, Singapore**
Printed by: **Dah Hua Printing Co. Ltd, Hong Kong**

PHOTOGRAPHS,
COVER AND
PRELIMINARY PAGES

Cover:
Gerbera jamesonii
cultivars

Page 1:
Aquilegia caerulea

Pages 2-3:
Leucanthemum x
superbum

Pages 4-5:
Digitalis purpurea

Pages 6-7:
Cyperus papyrus

Contents

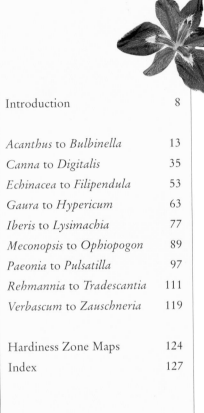

INTRODUCTION

PERENNIALS are a group of plants which live for at least three seasons, and may even live longer than many shrubs. In fact, many shrubs and trees are, strictly speaking, perennials, although the category generally excludes plants which develop a permanent woody stem or bark.

Perennials usually develop their foliage and root growth in the first growing season, and will only reach maturity, and produce flowers, in the second and subsequent seasons, before declining. Some plants, known as biennials, will produce a few flowers in their first year, and may be treated as annuals, which complete their whole life cycle (flower, set seed, and decline) all within one season.

Perennials are grown in climatic regions of all kinds, and as such, they have developed characteristics which allow them to adapt to their environment. Many herbaceous perennials, which account for most of the perennials in temperate zones, undergo a period of dormancy during winter months, when the above-ground foliage dies back to the crown, and the plant exists entirely as permanent root stock. In some hot, dry areas, this dormant period may occur in summer, or times of extremely low rainfall.

Some herbaceous perennials have further evolved the ability to lie dormant for extended periods, relying on storage roots for nutrition. These storage roots are

Dahlia (Dahlia, Group 5, 'Majuba' shown) tubers should be lifted and protected from winter frosts

known as tubers or rhizomes. The bearded iris is an example of a rhizomatous perennial, while dahlias and alstroemerias both form tuberous growths. In cold climates, dahlia tubers should be dug up and stored in a frost-free environment, before being split and replanted in the spring. Some rhizomes extend out from the parent plant, either just beneath the soil, or on the surface, developing new roots as they spread. It is no surprise, then, that it is possible to propagate perennials from rhizomes and tubers, with the added bonus that they will reach maturity—and flower—more rapidly than those grown from seed.

Phlox, lilies and erigeron daisies cause a riot in just two colors—white and pink

Use in the garden

In the garden, perennials take up where annuals leave off: like annuals, they 'flesh out' the green skeleton of a garden by providing color, variety and interest, but they have the advantage of a longer growing period. Perennials live for at least three years, but under the right conditions, and especially in cooler climates, they can stay in the garden permanently. Of course, some perennials are treated like annuals since they mature rapidly and are past their best after only one season.

Perennials are readily available, relatively inexpensive, and, with their wide range of growing characteristics, are the mainstay of the flower garden. In botanic gardens and parks, large drifts of perennials and annuals are grouped together with spectacular results, but even on a much smaller scale, perennials can surprise and delight the visitor to the smaller, private garden. Perennials usually flower at the same time every year, so it is possible to plan the garden so that one area comes into flower just as another, close by, is losing its appeal.

The riotous colors and exuberant growth of perennials contrast well with the uniform color and smooth texture of lawn, and, with a bit of careful planning, you can take advantage of the huge variety in height, form, foliage and flower to achieve a garden which gives pleasure all through the year.

Although there are no hard and fast rules about color combinations in the garden (just as the colors of cut flowers 'cannot clash'), it a good idea when planning a perennial bed, or herbaceous border, to restrict your palette to one or two colors, and shades of those colors. That way, your planting will have both visual impact and cohesion. The cottage garden and wildflower garden are exceptions, however, since it is their apparent freedom from planning wherein lies their appeal. Whatever your style, try to envisage the mature height and spread of the plants, planting the tallest ones towards the back of the bed, shorter ones towards the front, and allowing plenty of room for sideways growth.

Many perennials are renowned for their distinctive foliage or form, rather than for their floral display, and it can be very gratifying to group several such plants together, either as a border, or as an attractive backdrop to shorter plants. In the first season, small drifts of annuals may help fill in the gaps between the immature perennials.

Growing habits and effects

The cottage garden, wildflower garden, woodland garden, rock garden, formal, or semi-formal garden—all make use of the

The colors and textures of this mixed border contrast with the smooth green lawn beyond

myriad growing habits of perennials. For a cottage garden, choose old fashioned, simple varieties, such as *Coreopsis* or foxglove, and subtle colors, and avoid plants with masses of double, 'overdeveloped' flowers.

The 'natural look' of the wildflower garden, the woodland garden and the rock garden paradoxically demands meticulous planning, and the timing of planting is vital.

Perennials do very well in containers, and are often used in combination with annuals in tubs, window boxes and hanging baskets. Don't forget to use a good potting mix, and feed container plants regularly.

Starting out...and getting results

Most perennials can be grown from seed, but many can be propagated after the growing season by dividing an established crown or rhizome, and replanting, usually in spring. This not only shortens the time to flowering, but it also means that the results are predictable, since the new plant will produce flowers of the same color and type as the parent plant. Most perennials should be divided at least every 3 years, although some, such as the peony, will tolerate being left for longer, and will take a while to recover.

Some knowledge of a plant's origins will give clues about its needs, so it is worth getting to know your plants. Perennials from warmer climates, for example, will usually need protection from frost, while for some, even those which are quite frost hardy, the combination of cold and wet is deadly. In general, the aim should be to emulate the growing conditions the plant would encounter growing wild, although often a plant will respond very well to slightly kinder treatment.

Preparation of the garden bed for the planting of perennials is particularly important, since they are often left *in situ* for some years. Weed and then double dig the bed; that is, dig over the topsoil to a fork's depth, remove it to one side, and dig over the lower layer of soil, to the same depth.

Gerbera jamesonii *cultivars are relatively frost resistant, but tend to rot under cold and wet conditions*

At this stage, fork in some well-rotted manure or compost, which will improve the moisture-retaining properties of sandy soil, and will help break up clay particles. Then replace the topsoil and dig over, adding a complete fertilizer, well-rotted manure or compost.

When it comes to planting, there are just a few basic principles to consider: make holes a suitable distance apart using a dibble or pencil; separate the roots of seedlings carefully; and make sure that you plant seedlings at the same soil level as in the seed tray. After that, all you need to do is firm down the soil around each seedling, and water immediately. When planting a divided crown or rhizome, take care not to bury it too deeply; the top of the crown should be just below the soil surface.

Maintaining perennials involves regularly removing spent flowers and developing seed heads in order to prolong the blooming period, and tidying the foliage from time to time. Tall plants, such as dahlias, will need to be staked for support, and it is a good idea to put the stakes up at planting time, or you risk damaging the mature crown. At the end of summer, be ruthless about cutting back and removing the dead foliage.

Watering is best achieved using perforated soak hoses and drip lines, which control and direct watering and prevent damage to plants. Rain provides enough moisture for most spring-flowering perennials, unless the season is unusually dry, but regular watering throughout the season is vital for summer-flowering species. Containers, especially hanging baskets, need water daily, or even twice-daily, in hot weather.

Pests and diseases will vary depending on the plant and the climate, so if you suspect that your plants are suffering from the effects of either, it is advisable to seek professional help from your local garden center or nursery. In general, established plants growing in the correct conditions will be more resistant to pests and disease than those struggling to adapt to non-ideal conditions. Seedlings are vulnerable regardless, and may succumb to attack by snails, slugs, birds, cutworms, earwigs and slaters, and are prone to the fungal disease known as damping off, which causes them to collapse. For this reason, it is as well to drench seedlings with a fungicidal solution at regular intervals.

AB

ACANTHUS

Bear's breeches

This genus comprises around 30 species of perennials and shrubs from tropical Africa and Asia, as well as Mediterranean Europe. The genus name goes back to ancient Greek, and the family Acanthaceae takes its name from the genus. The carved motifs on the capitals of Corinthian columns echo the deeply lobed and toothed leaves of *Acanthus mollis* and the similar *A. spinosus*. Only the more temperate perennial species have been much cultivated, as much for their foliage as their tall spikes of bracted, distinctively shaped flowers. Flowers appear in spring and early summer, after which the leaves may die back before sprouting once again before winter.

CULTIVATION Frost hardy, they do best in full sun or light shade. They prefer a rich, well-drained soil with adequate moisture in winter and spring. Remove spent flower stems and leaves if preferred. Snails and caterpillars can damage the new leaves. Propagate by division in fall (autumn), or from seed.

Acanthus mollis

Occurring on both sides of the Mediterranean, this well-known species is somewhat variable, the

Acanthus mollis

form grown in gardens having broader, softer leaves and taller spikes than most wild plants. It likes shelter and deep moist soil, since it is more of a woodland plant than other acanthuses. Large, deep green, glossy leaves are quite soft and may droop in hot dry weather. Flower spikes, which can exceed 6 ft (1.8 m) in height, carry purple-pink bracts and crinkled white flowers. Spread is by deeply buried rhizomes, hence it may be hard to eradicate once established. **'Candelabrus'** is one of several cultivars.

ZONES 7–10.

ACHILLEA

Yarrow, milfoil, sneezewort

The name derives from Greek mythology, wherein Achilles used this plant to heal wounds. Of the more than 80 species of *Achillea*, most are native to Europe and temperate Asia, with a handful in North America. Foliage is fernlike, aromatic and often hairy. Most species bear masses of large, flat heads of tiny daisy flowers in shades of white, yellow, orange, pink or red, from late spring to fall (autumn). They are suitable for borders and rock gardens.

Achillea millefolium 'Apfelblute'

CULTIVATION These hardy perennials are tolerant of poor soils and are easy to grow, but they do prefer sunny, well-drained sites in temperate climates. They multiply rapidly by deep rhizomes and are easily propagated by division in late winter or from cuttings in early summer. Flowering stems may be cut when spent or left to die back on their own. Prune the clumps in winter to stimulate strong spring growth and fertilize in spring.

Achillea millefolium
Milfoil, yarrow

This common species, well known in Europe and temperate Asia, is hardy, extremely vigorous and naturalizes freely. It reaches 24 in (60 cm) in height, with soft, feathery, dark green foliage and white to pink flowers in summer. Cultivars bear flowers ranging from deep rose pink to orange-red, cherry red and rose red. Once established, plants can be difficult to eradicate. Most *Achillea* hybrids have this species as one parent.

ZONES 3–10.

Useful Tip

The dried flowerheads of Achillea *retain their color, so are popular in dried arrangements for winter decoration.*

ACONITUM
Aconite, monkshood, wolfsbane

This genus is renowned for the deadly poisons contained in the sap of many of its some 100 species of perennials, native to temperate regions of the northern hemisphere. From ancient times until quite recently they were used for deliberate poisoning, from execution of criminals to baiting wolves, or placing in an enemy's water supply. The poison has also been used medicinally in carefully controlled doses and is a subject of pharmaceutical research. The 5-petalled flowers are instantly recognizable: mostly in shades of deep blue or

Aconitum napellus

purple, or less commonly white, pink or yellow, they form a prominent helmet-like shape. The growth habit and leaves are similar to the delphinium, a relative.

CULTIVATION Aconites are suited to herbaceous borders and woodland gardens, prefering deep, moist soil and a sheltered position, partly shaded if summers are hot and dry. Propagate from seed or by division after the leaves die back in fall (autumn).

Aconitum napellus
Aconite, monkshood

This vigorous species, the most popular in gardens and as handsome as any, is well-known in Europe and temperate Asia. The erect stems reach 4 ft (1.2 m), with large leaves divided into very narrow segments and a tall, open spike of deep blue to purplish flowers. It likes damp woodland or stream bank conditions.

ZONES 5–9.

AGAPANTHUS
African lily, agapanthus, lily-of-the-Nile

Native to southern Africa, these vigorous perennials are popular for their fine foliage and their abundant, summer flowers. Arching, strap-like leaves spring from short rhizomes with dense, fleshy roots. Flowers are various shades of blue (white in some cultivars) in many flowered umbels, borne on a single erect stem, often 3 ft (1 m) in

Agapanthus praecox subsp. *orientalis*

height. Agapanthus is ideal as a backdrop for shorter plants or for planting alongside a wall, fence or driveway. Several hybrids exist.

CULTIVATION They thrive in conditions of neglect and on difficult sites such as dry slopes and near the coast. They prefer full sun but will tolerate some shade and will grow in any soil as long as they get water in spring and summer. They naturalize readily, soon forming large clumps; they also make excellent tub and container specimens. Trim off spent flower stems and dead leaves at the end of winter. They are frost hardy to marginally frost hardy. Propagate by division in late winter, or from seed in spring or fall (autumn).

Agapanthus praecox

This is the most popular agapanthus and often, plants sold as *A. africanus* turn out to be *A. praecox*. Its densely clumped, evergreen foliage is an asset throughout the year; the extravagant rounded umbels in lavender blue appear in summer. It is also available in white. *Agapanthus praecox* subsp. *orientalis* has large dense umbels of blue flowers. It prefers full sun, moist soil and is marginally frost hardy.

ZONES 9–11.

AJUGA

Bugle

About 50 species of low-growing annuals and perennials make up this genus, which ranges through Europe, Asia, Africa and Australia, mainly in cooler regions. Although belonging to the mint family, their foliage is barely aromatic. Rosettes of soft, spatulate leaves lengthen into spikes of blue, purple or pink (rarely yellow) 2-lipped flowers. Most perennial species spread by runners or underground rhizomes, some forming extensive carpets. They make attractive ground covers, especially for shady places such as corners of courtyards.

CULTIVATION These are frost-hardy, trouble-free plants requiring only moist soil and shelter from strong sun (though the bronze and variegated forms do best in sun). The popular species thrive in a range of climates, from severe cold to subtropical. Propagate by division. Watch for snails and slugs.

Useful Tip

Dry clove-scented Dianthus *blooms or aromatic* Tanacetum *foliage for your own pot pourri.*

Ajuga reptans
European bugle, common bugle, blue bugle

This species, native to Europe, spreads indefinitely by surface runners, making a mat of leafy rosettes only 2-3 in (5–8 cm) high. In spring it sends up spikes up to 8 in (20 cm) high of deep blue flowers. Several cultivars are grown for their leaf colors: **'Atropurpurea'** syn. **'Purpurea'** (dull purple to bronze-green); **'Burgundy Glow'** (cream and maroon variegated); **'Multicolor'** (white, pink and purple); **'Variegata'** (light green and cream); and **'Jungle Beauty'** (dark green tinged with purple). **'Catlin's Giant'** has much larger leaves and longer, to 8 in (20 cm),

inflorescences. **'Pink Elf'** is compact with dark pink flowers.

ZONES 3–10.

ALCHEMILLA
Lady's mantle

There are around 300 species of perennials in this genus which is distributed from arctic and north temperate zones, to the mountains of tropical Africa, India, Sri Lanka and Java. A few alpine species exist in Australia and New Zealand, but it is not clear if they are natives or naturalized imports. They form clumps of hand-shaped or rounded, lobed, gray-green leaves, often covered with silky hairs. Their spreading stems often root as they

Ajuga reptans

Alchemilla mollis

grow. Frothy sprays of tiny yellow-green flowers develop in summer. They range in size from 6–30 in (15–75 cm) tall and wide. Many species have styptic and other medicinal properties.

CULTIVATION They are very hardy and easily grown in any well-drained soil in afternoon shade. They will tolerate sun but the foliage will not withstand the summer heat. They are excellent for a wildflower or rock garden. Propagate from seed or division in late winter to early spring.

Alchemilla mollis
Lady's mantle

Sometimes sold as *Alchemilla vulgaris*, this is the most widely cultivated species in the genus. It is a low-growing, clump-forming perennial ideal for ground cover, the front of borders or for rock gardens. It grows to a height and spread of 16 in (40 cm). Its decorative, wavy-edged leaves hold dew or raindrops to give a sparkling effect. In summer, it bears masses of small sprays of greenish yellow flowers, similar to *Gypsophila*.

ZONES 4–9.

Useful Tip

 The masses of yellow-green miniature flowers, borne on good-sized stems, make Alchemilla mollis *popular for flower arrangements.*

ALSTROEMERIA

Peruvian lily

These plants are well loved as cut flowers, although they do tend to drop their petals. In all, there are about 50 species of these tuberous and rhizomatous plants which are native to the mountain scree and open grassland of South America. Tall, straight stems with scattered, thin and twisted leaves concentrated on the upper half end in umbels of outward-facing flowers, usually with flaring petals that are variously spotted or streaked. Flowers are borne in profusion from spring to summer.

CULTIVATION All thrive in sun or light shade in a well-enriched, well-drained acidic soil medium. They soon form large clumps with masses of flowerheads. Propagate from seed or by division in early spring. They are frost hardy, but in cold winters protect the dormant tubers by covering with loose peat or dry bracken. Best left undis-

Alstroemeria, Ligtu Hybrids

turbed when established, but one-year-old seedlings transplant well. Alstroemerias do well naturalized under trees or on sloping banks.

Alstroemeria ligtu
St Martin's flower

This Chilean species is one of the more cold-hardy species. Growing 24–36 in (60–90 cm) tall, it has very narrow leaves and large compound umbels of lilac, orange or red flowers with purple or white streaks or spots. The Ligtu Hybrids first appeared in Britain in the late 1920s, when *Alstroemeria ligtu* was crossed with *A. haemantha*. Colors range from cream to orange, red and yellow, but the plants die soon after flowering. Other hybrid strains derived from *A. aurea* have recently superseded them as popular cut flowers.

ZONES 7–9.

ANEMONE
Windflower

This genus of over 100 species of perennials occurs widely in the northern hemisphere, but with the majority in temperate Asia. Species include a diverse range of woodland plants as well as the common florist's anemone (*Anemone coronaria*). All have tufts of basal leaves that are divided in palmate fashion into few to many leaflets. The saucer- or bowl-shaped flowers have 5 or more petals and a central boss of stamens, and come in almost every color. Anemones can be divided into species with fibrous roots, which flower in the fall (autumn), and tuberous and rhizomatous species, usually spring flowering. Given the right conditions and left undisturbed for many years, many of these will form wonderful carpets of both texture and color. The tuberous types (*A. coronaria* being the best known) are best replaced every 1–2 years.

Anemone hupehensis 'Hadspen Abundance'

CULTIVATION Most woodland species are very frost hardy and do well in rich, moist yet well-drained soil in a lightly shaded position. Propagate from seed planted in summer or divide established clumps in early winter when plant is dormant. The tuberous types do well in full sun and well-drained soil and welcome a dry dormancy period. However, they are more prone to frost damage and the tubers tend to become weakened after blooming. For this reason, they are often treated as annuals.

Anemone hupehensis
Japanese windflower

Originally from China, but long cultivated in Japan, this fibrous-rooted perennial can be almost evergreen in milder climates. If conditions are to its liking, it may spread and provide good ground cover, producing its single white to mauve flowers on tall, openly branched stems during the early fall (autumn). Cultivars may have pale or deep pink petals, while *Anemone hupehensis* var. *Japonica*, the Japanese cultivated race, is taller and has more petals than the Chinese plants. Most cultivars ascribed to this species are now placed under *Anemone* x *hybrida*.

ZONES 6–10.

ANIGOZANTHOS
Kangaroo paw, cat's paw

These evergreen perennials have distinctive tubular flowers, the outsides of which are densely hairy, and which open at the top to form 'claws'; the whole supposedly resembles a kangaroo's paw.

Anigozanthos humilis

Birds are attracted to these plants, which are native to southwestern Australia. Foliage is somewhat grass-like and species vary in height from 1–6 ft (30 cm–1.8 m). Flowers come in many colors including green, gold, deep red and orange-red; some species and hybrids are bicolored. In recent years many hybrids have been developed for the cut-flower industry and the florists' trade in potted flowers, although most will grow outdoors equally well.

CULTIVATION They prefer warm, very well-drained sandy or gravelly soil and a hot, sunny, open position. Water well during dry seasons. Most will tolerate very light frosts and do well in coastal regions. Most tolerate drought, although flowering will be prolonged with summer water. Propagate by division in spring or from fresh seed. Plants are often affected by ink disease, a fungus which blackens the foliage. Watch for snails.

Anigozanthos humilis
Common cat's paw

This is a low, clumping perennial, growing no taller than 15 in (40 cm) but spreading anything up to 3 ft (1 m) if conditions are favorable. It can die back in summer and fall (autumn), so don't allow it to be overgrown while dormant. The flowering stems, often twice the height of the foliage, carry blooms in a wide range of colors from cream through dull orange to red. It prefers full sun.

ZONES 9-11.

ANTHEMIS

Under ideal conditions, the 100 or so species of this genus of annuals and perennials from Mediterranean regions and western Asia flower prolifically, and over a prolonged season, from late spring to late summer. Belonging to the larger daisy family, the flowerheads have the typical daisy shape and are generally white, cream or yellow with distinctive contrasting disc florets. Aside from the attractive flowers, most species have somewhat aromatic,

Anthemis tinctoria

filigree foliage in shades of green or silver gray, which is of value in the mixed border or rockery. Formerly *Anthemis* included the herbal chamomile, which belongs to the genus *Chamaemelum*.

CULTIVATION These plants flower best in full sun and like well-drained soil. The perennials can be short-lived and often become untidy, but cutting back after flowering in the fall (autumn) ensures a more shapely plant. They are easily replaced by cuttings taken in the warmer months or by division in fall (autumn) or spring. Annual species can be grown from seed.

Anthemis tinctoria
Dyer's chamomile, golden marguerite

The epithet 'tinctoria' signifies a dye plant, and indeed the flowers of this species can be used to make a yellow dye. Native to Europe and western Asia, this is a very hardy, easily grown perennial that is covered in late spring and summer with a dazzling display of daisy flowers above fern-like, crinkled green leaves. The flowers are bright golden; cultivars, notably **'E. C. Buxton'** have more subtle soft yellow blooms and fine foliage. The plant can achieve a height of 3 ft (1 m) with the support of a rockery or a bank.

ZONES 4–10.

AQUILEGIA
Columbine

The common name comes from the Latin for dove, coined since the flowers bear a resemblance to a cluster of doves. Native to Europe, North America and temperate regions of Asia, these graceful,

Aquilegia caerulea

clump-forming perennials are grown for their spurred, bell-shaped flowers of varied colors, and for their fern-like foliage. Single and double forms exist. While some taller species are popular as cut flowers, the dwarf and alpine species are suitable for rock gardens. Columbines tend to flower in late spring and early summer, and look best in clumps with annuals in the foreground.

CULTIVATION They are frost hardy, but prefer a sunny site protected from strong winds and with some shade in hot areas. They like well-drained, light soil, enriched with manure. In cold climates columbines are perennials and need to be cut back to the ground in late winter, but treat larger-flowered cultivars as annuals for best results. Propagation is by division or from seed in fall (autumn) and spring, although many self-seed readily.

Aquilegia caerulea
Blue columbine, Rocky Mountain columbine

Arguably the finest of the wild columbines, this is the state flower of Colorado. It is a short-lived, upright, alpine species from the Rocky Mountains, reaching 24 in (60 cm) or more in height, with a rather narrow growth habit. Large, powdery blue and white nodding flowers on branching stems appear in late spring and early summer; a few blooms may appear in fall (autumn). It does best in rich soil.

ZONES 3–9.

ARENARIA
Sandwort

This genus comprises around 160 species of mainly low growing perennials, some of them evergreen, some becoming shrubby with age. They are widespread in the northern hemisphere, with a few southern hemisphere species too. The plants commonly develop a dense mass of fine stems clothed with tiny, deep green or

Arenaria montana

gray-green leaves and small, usually white, flowers in spring or summer. The flowers may be borne singly or in small clusters. Several mound-forming species are ideal for filling cracks in paving or a wall, for rock gardens and for containers.

CULTIVATION They are easily grown in any moist, well-drained soil in full sun. They are not troubled by pests or disease, and are generally very frost hardy. Propagate from seed, self-rooted layers or small tip cuttings.

Arenaria montana

A native of southwest Europe, this species is larger than most in both leaves and flowers. It has gray-green leaves up to 1½ in (35 mm) long and mounds up to about 6 in (15 cm). Its flowering stems tend to be erect and extend slightly above the foliage clump. Flowers, 1 in (25 mm) across, are pure white with yellow–green centers, and are abundant.

ZONES 4–9.

Useful Tip

Deadhead perennials regularly to prolong their flowering season, and to keep the plants looking their best.

ARMERIA

Thrift, sea pink

This genus of about 35 species of low-growing, tufted perennials grows in a wide variety of environments—from salt marshes and storm-swept headlands to alpine meadows—in the temperate zones of Eurasia, Africa and the Americas. The crowded, narrow, mostly evergreen leaves usually form a dense mound; in early summer, small flowers crowd into globular heads, each atop a slender stalk.

Armeria alliacea

Armeria maritima

CULTIVATION They are suitable for rock gardens or borders and prefer exposed, sunny positions and rather dry soil with good drainage. They are generally frost hardy. Propagate from seed or cuttings in spring or fall (autumn). *Armeria maritima*, the common thrift, is native to much of the northern hemisphere, and consists of many wild races. It has been cultivated since 1578, and most cultivars are derived from this species.

Armeria alliacea

This is a particularly robust species, which comes from the mountains of western Europe. Large tufts of long, soft, flat, deep green leaves contrast with numerous bright reddish purple flowerheads on stems up to 18 in (45 cm) tall.

ZONES 5–9.

ASTER

Michaelmas or Easter daisy, aster

Over 250 species belong in this genus of perennials and deciduous or evergreen subshrubs, native to temperate regions of the northern hemisphere (most in North America). They range from miniatures, perfect for rock gardens, to 6 ft (1.8 m) giants. The simple leaves are mostly smooth edged, sometimes hairy, often quite small. Showy, daisy-like flowerheads are usually produced in late summer or fall (autumn) in blue, violet, purple, pink, red and white, all with a central disc of yellow or purple. Many cultivars, once listed under the parent species, now stand alone. A typical example is

Aster 'Coombe's Violet'. The 'China asters' now belong in the genus *Callistephus*.

CULTIVATION Easy to grow, they prefer sun (or part-shade in hot areas) and a well-drained, compost-enriched soil. Protect from strong wind, stake the taller specimens, and keep moist. When the flowers fade, cut the stems back to ground level and tidy the clumps. Propagate by division in spring or late fall (autumn), or take softwood cuttings in spring. Divide plants every 2-3 years, using the most vigorous outer part. Powdery mildew, rust, aphids and snails can be a problem.

Aster ericoides
Heath aster

This species from eastern and central USA and northern Mexico has very small, narrow leaves, at least on the upper stems, which resemble *Erica*. Flowering stems rise up to 3 ft (1 m) from tufted basal shoots from mid-summer into fall (autumn), providing a wonderful display of massed, small, white flowerheads. **'White Heather'** is a compact cultivar. Other cultivars are of varied heights, mostly with pale pinkish or yellowish blooms. The cut flowers are popular with florists.

ZONES 4–10.

Aster ericoides

ASTILBE

False spiraea

This genus of 14 species of early to late summer perennials comes mostly from eastern Asia, where they favor moist ground beside woodland streams; 2 species occur in the eastern USA. All astilbes have basal tufts of ferny, compound leaves, the leaflets usually sharply toothed. Pointed, plume-like panicles of tiny, white to pink or red flowers rise clear above the tuft. Most commonly cultivated are the hybrids of the group *Astilbe* x *arendsii*. The name 'spiraea' was mistakenly attached to this genus when they were introduced to England in the 1820s.

CULTIVATION They thrive in light shade and rich, leafy soil that never dries out, though they do not like being flooded, especially in cold weather. They do best in cooler climates; keep their roots cool in hot summers by constant watering. They make good cut flowers, and pretty indoor pot plants while

Astilbe, Arendsii Hybrid, 'Europa'

Astilbe, Arendsii Hybrid, 'Fanal'

blooming. In a heated greenhouse they will flower early. Propagate by division in winter.

Astilbe, **Arendsii Hybrids**

This hybrid group, derived from four east Asian species, is named after German horticulturist Georg Arends (1863–1952), responsible for many of the finest cultivars. Heights vary from 18-48 in (45 cm–1.2 m), with a spread of 18-30 in (45–75 cm). Feathery spikes appear in late spring to early summer. Cultivars range in colors from red through pink to white.

ZONES 6–10.

AUBRIETA

Rock cress

The genus name, sometimes given as *Aubrietia,* honors the French botanical painter Claude Aubriet (1668-1743). Although mountain flowers, aubrietas are not diminutive and difficult as are many alpines. Only about 6 in (15 cm) high at most, they form carpets of color at the front of flowerbeds, or down retaining walls, happily sprawling to several times their height. In spring they are a mass of 4-petalled, mainly purple, flowers. About a dozen species are native to stony hillsides and mountains of the Mediterranean area, as far east as Iran. The plants commonly seen in gardens are hybrids mainly derived from *Aubrieta deltoidea*.

CULTIVATION Easy to grow in cool-temperate climates (flowering is erratic in warm ones), these short-lived plants need only sunshine or a little shade and rich, well-drained soil. Take cuttings in summer every 3 or 4 years, or propagate by division of the rhizomatous rootstock.

Aubrieta deltoidea

A native of southeastern Europe and Turkey, this perennial forms a compact mat of gray-green leaves and bears masses of starry, mauve pink flowers over a long period in spring. Since most cultivated aubrietas are hybrids known collectively as *Aubrieta* x *cultorum* (commonly listed as *A. deltoidea*), the species is now rarely seen in gardens.

ZONES 4–9.

AURINIA

This genus of 7 species of biennials and evergreen perennials was formerly included in *Alyssum*, whose origins are in central and southern Europe to the Ukraine and Turkey. They are mainly small, spreading, clump-forming plants. Leaves initially form basal rosettes and are fairly narrow, spoon- or inversely lance-shaped. They bear elongated sprays of tiny yellow or white flowers in spring and early summer.

CULTIVATION Plant in light, gritty, well-drained soil in full sun. They are ideal for rockeries, rock crevices or dry-stone walls. Most species are very frost hardy and can be propagated from seed or small tip cuttings, though they will self-sow in suitable locations.

Aubrieta deltoidea

Useful Tip

To propagate yellow alyssum, root softwood cuttings in the early summer, or sow seeds in a cold frame in the fall (autumn).

Aurinia saxatilis

syn. *Alyssum saxatile*

Basket of gold, yellow alyssum

This native to central and south-eastern Europe is the only commonly grown species and is very popular as a rockery or wall plant. Its hairy, gray-green leaves form fairly loose mounds, not more than 10 in (25 cm) high, which are smothered in bright yellow flowers in spring and early summer. A number of cultivars exist: **'Argentea'** with very silvery leaves; **'Citrina'** with lemon yellow flowers; **'Gold Dust'**, with 12 in (30 cm) mounds and deep golden yellow flowers; **'Sulphurea'** with glowing yellow flowers; and **'Tom Thumb'**, a 4 in (10 cm) dwarf with small leaves.

ZONES 4–9.

Aurinia saxatilis

BERGENIA

Elephant-eared saxifrage, elephant's ears

This genus, from eastern and central Asia, comprises 6 or 7 species of rhizomatous, semi-evergreen perennials in the saxifrage family. It is characterised by large, handsome, paddle-shaped leaves which arise from the ground on short stalks to form loose clumps. The foliage often develops attractive red tints in winter. Large clusters of flowers—mostly pale pink, but also white and dark pink—are borne on short, stout stems in winter and spring. Many garden hybrids have been developed over the last century or so, including **'Eroica'**, with deep pink flowers.

Bergenia cordifolia

CULTIVATION They make excellent rockery plants. They thrive in both sun and shade and are tolerant of exposed sites as well as moist ground beside streams or ponds, but the foliage color is deeper in drier sites. Some are good as ground cover when planted *en masse*. Water well in hot weather and remove spent flowerheads to prolong flowering. Propagate by division in spring after flowering, when plants become crowded.

Bergenia cordifolia
Heartleaf saxifrage

Native to Siberia's Altai Mountains, this tough perennial has crinkly-edged, more or less heart-shaped leaves up to 8 in (20 cm) wide, and produces panicles of drooping purple-pink flowers on 12-15 in (30–38 cm) stems in late winter and early spring. It has a prolonged flowering season and its leaves remain green in winter. **'Purpurea'** has magenta-pink flowers and leaves tinged purple.

ZONES 3–9.

Bergenia 'Morgenröte'
syn. 'Morning Red'

A small, clump-forming cultivar, with plain green broad leaves, 5-6 in (13-15 cm) long. Bright orchid pink flowers are held on deep red stalks in late spring. May bloom again in cool summers.

ZONES 4-9.

Bergenia 'Silberlicht'
syn. 'Silver Light'

A hybrid cultivar, the glossy green leaves of which form compact clumps. The leaves have scalloped edges and reach 8 in (20 cm) in

Bergenia 'Morgenröte'

Bergenia 'Silberlicht'

length. A succession of 18 in (45 cm) flower stalks bear clusters of large, pure white to palest pink flowers in late spring.

ZONES 5–9.

BULBINELLA

Six of the 20 or so species in this genus are endemic to New Zealand; the rest are native to southern Africa. They are fleshy-rooted perennial lilies similar to the related *Bulbine* but with mostly broader, thinner leaves and long, hollow stems terminating in crowded spikes of golden yellow flowers. They form clumps of somewhat untidy foliage. Some of the larger South African species make excellent cut flowers. The alpine species are not as easy to grow, and are much smaller.

CULTIVATION In the wild, many species grow in very damp areas and in the garden, they demand moist, humus-rich soil that never dries out entirely in summer. They do best in full sun or semi-shade. Most species are at least slightly frost hardy and are propagated from seed or by dividing established clumps. The fleshy roots should be planted with the root-crown at soil level.

Bulbinella floribunda
Cat's-tail

This native of South Africa produces 24–36 in (60–90 cm) tall flower stalks from late winter to mid-spring. Each stalk is topped by a broad, 4 in (10 cm) spike crammed with tiny orange-yellow flowers and tight green buds at the tip. Long, narrow basal leaves appear in winter, forming a large tangled clump. The plant dies back in summer and fall (autumn). It is excellent as a long-lasting cut flower.

ZONES 8-10.

Bulbinella floribunda

CD

CANNA

Indian shot plant

About 25 species of vigorous rhizomatous perennials originating from tropical and South America make up this genus. Members of the same broad group as gingers and bananas, they too have false stems made up of tightly furled leaf bases, rising from the thick knotty rhizomes. Flowering stems grow up through the centers of the false stems, emerging at the top with (usually) a pair of asymmetrical flowers. Although most wild cannas have narrow-petalled flowers in yellow, red or purple, garden hybrids (developed in the mid-nineteenth century) have broader petals and recent hybrids, 'orchid-flowered cannas', bear larger crumpled flowers with striking variegations. Colors range from common reds, oranges and yellows to apricots, creams and pinks. Leaves may be green, bronze or purple, even white- or yellow-striped. Plants range in height from 18 in-8 ft (45 cm-2.4 m).

CULTIVATION Cannas thrive in frost-free, warm climates but in colder areas the roots need to be

Useful Tip

In frost-prone areas, after a frost in fall (autumn) has discolored the canna leaves, cut back the stems and leaves and lift the rhizome. Store in leaf mold or just-moist peat until spring.

Canna x *generalis* 'Königin Charlotte'

protected with thick mulch in winter, or else the rhizomes may be lifted in fall (autumn) and stored until spring. They can also be grown indoors in a conservatory. They are sun-loving, thriving in hot dry weather as long as water can be kept up to the roots, and they respond well to heavy feeding. Cut back to the ground after flowers finish. Propagate in spring by division.

Canna x generalis

This group of hybrids includes dwarfs less than 3 ft (1 m) and plants as tall as 6 ft (1.8 m). Foliage may be plain green, reddish, purple or variegated, and flowers come in all the warm shades, either in plain single colors, or spotted or streaked. **'Königin Charlotte'** has dazzling red flowers.

ZONES 9–12.

Canna x *generalis*

CHRYSANTHEMUM

The once large and varied genus of *Chrysanthemum* has been the subject of much debate over the years. Once it contained not only the florists' chrysanthemums but several other related groups such as the shasta daisies, marguerites, tansies and pyrethrums. For a while, florists' chrysanthemums were given their own genus, Dendranthema, but a recent decision by an international committee on botanical nomenclature has brought their scientific name back into line with popular usage and they have now had the name *Chrysanthemum* restored to them. The painted daisy, corn marigold and crown daisy will soon be split off to form their own genus (likely to be *Dendranthema*); in the meantime, however, they retain the genus name '*Chrysanthemum*', but in quotes.

CULTIVATION Mostly frost hardy, these plants prefer a sunny site and well-drained, slightly acidic soil. Pinch off lateral buds to promote the central flower, and stake tall plants. Propagate from seed, by division, or cuttings.

Classified by flower form, the 10 main groups are:

Anemone-centered: Daisy-like flower with a pin cushion center and single or double ray of radiating flat florets. Grown as a spray.

Chrysanthemum x *grandiflorum, single form*

Incurved: Fully double globular bloom formed of incurving tightly packed florets. They last well and are used as cut flowers and for shows.

Intermediate: Fully double blooms with incurving, shaggy form, and sometimes outcurving basal florets.

Pompon: Fully double globular blooms, normally grown in sprays. Good cut flowers.

Quill-shaped: Double blooms with narrow tubular florets opening at the tips.

Reflexed: Rounded double blooms, with florets curving out and down, often twisted.

Fully reflexed: Perfectly rounded, double blooms, with florets curving out and down, lower ones touching the stem.

Single: Daisy-like blooms with up to 5 rows of radiating florets around a flat central disc. Ideal for massed planting; available in many colors.

Spiders: Double blooms with long, narrow tubular florets fanning out in all directions.

Spoon-shaped: Double blooms with very narrow radiating florets. The tips are expanded to form a spoon shape.

Chrysanthemum x *grandiflorum*

syns *Chrysanthemum morifolium, Dendranthema* x *grandiflorum*
Florists' chrysanthemum

Thought to be of Chinese origin, this hybrid has given rise to hundreds of cultivars categorized according to type of bloom, each of which has the full range of colors. A vigorous subshrub up to 5 ft (1.5 m) tall, it has thick, aromatic lobed leaves with a gray felted underside. The single flowers have a yellow center and spreading ray florets in white, pink or yellow through various bronze colors to deep red or purple. A recent development is the 'Korean chrysanthemum' which is a compact plant with smaller single heads, good for bedding.

ZONES 4-10.

Useful Tip

Dry the leaves and flowerheads of suitable plants by tying them in small bunches and hanging them in a warm, well ventilated spot out of direct sunlight, such as an airing cupboard, garage or a covered verandah.

Clivia miniata

CLIVIA

Kaffir lily

This genus of southern African lilies was named after Lady Clive, Duchess of Northumberland, granddaughter of Clive of India. She was a patron of gardening and *Clivia nobilis* first flowered in the UK in her greenhouses. There are 4 species of evergreen perennials with thick, strap-like, deep green leaves springing from short rhizomes with thick roots. Slightly flattened stems terminate in dense umbels, the flowers being funnel- or trumpet-shaped, with 6 red to orange, sometimes green-tipped petals that are partially fused into a tube. Deep red, berry-like fruits may follow flowering. *Clivia miniata* is the most popular species.

CULTIVATION They grow well outdoors in a mild, frost-free climate, or in a conservatory or greenhouse in regions with colder climates. Plant in a shaded or part-shaded position in friable, well-drained soil. They are surface rooting, however, and dislike soil disturbance. Keep fairly dry in winter and increase watering in spring and summer. Propagate by division after flowering. Clivias may also be grown from seed, but can be slow to flower.

Clivia miniata
Bush lily, fire lily

This most commonly cultivated and showiest species is distributed widely in eastern South Africa. About 18 in (45 cm) in height, it has broad leaves as much as 3 in (8 cm) wide and in spring, bears clusters of funnel-shaped flowers up to 3 in (8 cm) long, mostly orange to scarlet with a yellow throat. The occasional bloom may appear at other times. Many cultivars have been selected over the years, including yellow and cream forms, and a group of especially prized forms commonly called 'hybrids' have tulip-shaped, deep scarlet blooms. All parts of the plant cause stomach upset if ingested, and the sap is a skin irritant.

ZONES 10–11.

Useful Tip

For a deliciously fragrant garden, find a spot for Convallaria majus, *clove-scented* Dianthus, Hosta plantaginea, Paeonia lactiflora *hybrids and cultivars of* Phlox paniculata.

CONVALLARIA
Lily-of-the-valley

Although some botanists recognize several species of *Convallaria*, most believe there is only one, occurring wild in forests from France to Siberia and the cooler parts of North America. The plant spreads over the forest floor by slender underground rhizomes which at intervals send up dull green,

Convallaria majalis

pointed oval leaves and slender flowering stems adorned with little white bells. The red berries that follow have their uses in medicine, but, though sweet enough to tempt children, they are poisonous.

CULTIVATION The rhizomes, or 'pips' as they are commonly known from their growing tips, should be planted in fall (autumn) in a part-shaded position in moist and fertile, well-drained soil. Given the right conditions, it spreads freely and if it becomes overcrowded in a confined space, will benefit from lifting and thinning. They can be grown in pots for display indoors especially in warmer climates where they do poorly outdoors, or in cooler climates, when they can be replanted outdoors after flowering. Propagate from seed or by division.

Convallaria majalis

Renowned for its glorious perfume, this beautiful plant does best in cool climates. It is low growing, 8–12 in (20–30 cm) high, but of indefinite spread. It has mid-green leaves and bears dainty white, bell-shaped flowers, ¼-½ in (6–12 mm) across, in spring. Pink-flowered variants are collectively referred to as *Convallaria majalis* var. *rosea,* and there are several cultivars with variegated or gold foliage.

ZONES 3–9.

CONVOLVULUS

Found in many temperate regions of the world, the genus includes slender, twining creepers and small herbaceous plants. Only a few are shrubby, and even these are soft-stemmed and renewed by shooting from the base. The leaves are simple, thin-textured, often narrow and the flowers have a strongly flared tube that opens by unfurling 'pleats'. Convolvulus flowers stay open all day unlike morning glories (*Ipomoea*), which shrivel by mid-morning or early afternoon. Flowers usually open in succession over a long season.

CULTIVATION Easy to grow and tolerant of most soils and sites (exposed as well as sheltered), they

Convolvulus sabatius

prefer full sun. Cut back hard after flowering to promote thicker growth. Propagate from cuttings.

Convolvulus sabatius
syn. *Convolvulus mauritanicus*
Moroccan glory vine, bindweed, ground morning glory

Widely distributed in northern Africa with a foothold in southern Italy, this densely-trailing perennial has small oval leaves and a profusion of lilac-blue flowers from spring to fall (autumn). It has slender underground rhizomes, and its stems may twine around twigs. Excellent for draping over walls and hanging baskets, it grows to

Coreopsis lanceolata 'Baby Sun'

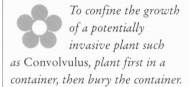

Useful Tip

To confine the growth of a potentially invasive plant such as Convolvulus, *plant first in a container, then bury the container.*

a height of 6-8 in (15–20 cm) and spreads extensively.

ZONES 8–11.

COREOPSIS

Some 80 species of annuals and perennials, from cooler or drier regions of the Americas, make up this genus of the daisy family. Flowerheads borne on slender stems mainly in summer are mostly shades of gold or yellow; some are bicolored. Leaves vary from simple, narrow and toothed, to deeply divided and may be basal or scattered up the stems.

CULTIVATION The annuals are grown as bedding plants, while the perennials are excellent for herbaceous borders. Perennials prefer full sun and a fertile, well-drained soil but also grow well in coastal regions and in poor, stony soil. Propagate by dividing old clumps in winter or spring, or by spring cuttings. Annuals also prefer full sun and a fertile, well-drained soil; they will not tolerate heavy clay soil. Stake tall varieties. Propagate from seed in spring or fall (autumn).

Coreopsis lanceolata

This tufted perennial has long-stalked, lance-shaped basal leaves and solitary bright yellow flower-heads borne on stems up to 24 in (60 cm) tall. It flowers profusely, and mass plantings produce sheets of color in spring and early summer. It is short-lived, but very free seeding, and is a weed in parts of Australia. Double forms are some

times grown. **'Baby Sun'** is a compact long blooming cultivar about 12 in (30 cm) high, suitable for bedding.

ZONES 3–11.

CYPERUS

Umbrella sedge, papyrus

Cyperus is an enormous genus of over 600 species of sedges found mainly in wet habitats in nearly all except the coldest parts of the

Cyperus papyrus

world. The broad clumps of thick, cylindrical or 3-angled stems have grass-like leaves springing from the base, and are topped by compact heads or large umbels of small chaff-like flower spikes.

CULTIVATION Most ornamental species do well at the water's edge or in boggy ground. Grow in rich compost and water well. Direct sunlight is tolerated. Repot when the plant fills the container. If the tips turn brown, the atmosphere may be too dry, while a lack of new stems may indicate too little light. Propagate from seed or by division.

Cyperus papyrus
Egyptian paper rush, paper reed, papyrus

Ancient Egyptians flattened and dried the stems of this magnificent water plant to make a form of paper. Suited to mild climates, it is extremely rampant, reaching 5-8 ft (1.5–2.4 m) in height, with an indefinite spread. In summer, its long, sturdy, leafless stems carry great starbursts of fine branchlets that carry the tiny brown flowers. It grows in very shallow water, preferring a sunny position.

ZONES 10–12.

DAHLIA

Of the 30 or so species in this genus from Mexico and Central America, only 2 or 3 were used to create thousands of named varieties. Hybrids are classified into about 10 different groups, according to the size and type of their flowerheads; most groups have small-, medium- and large-flowered subdivisions.

CULTIVATION They are fairly frost tender, so in cold areas lift the tubers and overwinter in a frost-

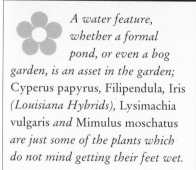

Useful Tip

A water feature, whether a formal pond, or even a bog garden, is an asset in the garden; Cyperus papyrus, Filipendula, Iris *(Louisiana Hybrids),* Lysimachia vulgaris *and* Mimulus moschatus *are just some of the plants which do not mind getting their feet wet.*

Dahlia, Group 5, 'Golden Ballade'

free place, then split and replant in spring. Most prefer a sunny, sheltered position and well-fertilized, well-drained soil. Feed monthly and water well when in flower, and stake all but bedding forms. Pinch out the lateral buds to promote growth of the central bud. Propagate bedding forms from seed; others from seed, tuber cuttings or by division.

The hybrid groups are as follows:

Single-flowered (Group 1): Single ray (or 2) of petals with an open center. Mostly small, so ideal for bedding.

Anemone-flowered (Group 2): One or more rows of outer ray florets; instead of the yellow center, these tiny flowers have outward-pointing tubular florets.

Collarette (Group 3): One row of 8 outer large florets, often flat and rounded at the tips, an inner row of shorter tubular, wavy florets (often in a contrasting color) and the normally yellow center.

Waterlily or nymphaea-flowered (Group 4): Fully double-flowered with slightly cupped petals, resembling waterlilies. The flower is fairly flat.

Decorative (Group 5): Fully double-flowered with no central disc showing. The petals are more numerous and slightly twisted, so

the flower looks fuller than Group 4 types, and there are some truly giant forms. Further subdivided into formal and informal types. Informal decoratives have twisted or pointed petals and an irregular arrangement. **'Golden Ballade'** is a large informal decorative dahlia; deep red **'Majuba'** is a medium-sized, free-flowering decorative.

Ball (Group 6): Full double flowers and almost ball shaped. Miniature, small, medium and large forms exist.

Pompon (Group 7): Similar to ball dahlias but even more globose and usually not much more than 2 in (5 cm) across. Sometimes called 'Drum Stick' dahlias.

Cactus (Group 8): Fully double with long, narrow rolled petals, giving a spidery look. Further subdivided by size and whether petals are straight, incurved or recurved.

Semi-cactus (Group 9): Similar to cactus dahlias but the petals are broader at the base and less rolled back at the edges.

Miscellaneous (Group 10): Consists of small groups and unique forms that do not fit into any other group: orchid types (single with revolute petals); star (single with pointed, widely spaced petals); and peony-flowered (1-2 rows of flat petals with a center either open or partly covered by small twisted petals).

DELPHINIUM

Most of the 250 or so species belong in temperate zones, mainly of the northern hemisphere, with a few found at high altitude in Africa. The range includes self-seeding annuals, dwarf alpine plants and tall perennials that can exceed 8 ft (2.4 m). Nearly all start growth as a tuft of long-stalked basal leaves, their blades divided into 3 to 7 radiating lobes or segments. The tufts elongate into erect, sometimes branched flowering stems that bear stalked, 5-petalled flowers, each with a backward-pointing nectar spur. Recognized groups include the Belladonna, Elatum and Pacific hybrids.

CULTIVATION Very frost hardy, most like a cool to cold winter. They prefer full sun with shelter from strong winds, and well-drained, fertile soil with plenty of organic matter. Stake tall plants. Apply a liquid fertilizer at 2–3 weekly intervals. Propagate from cuttings or by division. Some species have been bred true from seed.

Delphinium elatum hybrid 'Tempelgong'

Delphinium, Elatum Group

This group, whose main parent is *Delphinium elatum*, includes most of the tall delphiniums with flowers at least 2½ in (6 cm) across, tightly packed on a (usually unbranched) flower stem. They bloom from summer to fall (autumn) and are excellent for picking. Cut back after the first stems are spent, to encourage more, shorter stems. Numerous cultivars exist, bred for their specific flower color or form.

ZONES 3–9.

Useful Tip

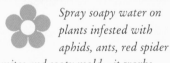

Spray soapy water on plants infested with aphids, ants, red spider mites and sooty mold—it works wonders as a fungicide and pesticide.

DIANTHUS

Carnation, pink

Most of the some 300 species occur in Europe and Asia, with one species in Arctic North America and a few in southern Africa. Most are rock garden or edging plants. Hybrids have been bred for particular purposes: Border Carnations, used in borders and for cut flowers; Perpetual-flowering Carnations and American Spray Carnations, often grown under cover for cut flowers; perfumed Malmaison Carnations, named after the Bourbon rose **'Souvenir de la Malmaison'** which they resemble; Modern Pinks and Old-fashioned Pinks bred for cutting and the garden; and Alpine or Rock Pinks, used mostly in rock gardens. In all groups, some

Dianthus, Modern Pink, 'Dick Portman'

cultivars are self-colored; others are flecked, picotee or laced; the latter two types with petals edged in a different color. The name 'pink' refers to the ragged edge of the petals, which look as if they have been cut with pinking shears.

CULTIVATION Varying from fully to marginally frost hardy, they like a sunny site, protection from strong winds, and well-drained, slightly alkaline soil. Stake taller varieties. Prune stems after flowering. Propagate perennials by layering or from cuttings in summer; annuals and biennials from seed in fall (autumn) or early spring. Watch for aphids, thrips and caterpillars, rust and virus infections.

Dianthus, Modern Pinks

Hybrids of *Dianthus plumarius* and *D. caryophyllus* cultivars (early examples called *D.* x *all-woodii*), these densely-leafed, mound-forming perennials have gray-green foliage and many erect flowering stems, each carrying 4-6, single to fully double flowers in

Dianthus, Perpetual-flowering Carnation, 'Sofia'

white, pink or crimson, often with dark centers and plain or fringed petals. Most are 12-18 in (30–45cm) tall, spreading 18 in (45 cm)and flowering from late spring until early fall (autumn); some are clove-scented.

ZONES 5–10.

Dianthus, Perpetual-flowering Carnations

These marginally frost hardy perennials reach at least 3 ft (1 m) high with a spread of 12 in (30 cm); their stems need support. Fully double blooms, usually fringed, are produced all year. Large-flowered types need dis-budding; spray types do not.

ZONES 8–11.

DIASCIA

Twinspur

Valued for their long flowering season, this genus of about 50 species of delicate perennials from

Diascia rigescens

South Africa is popular in rockeries, borders and containers. Erect or prostrate stems with toothed leaves bear terminal racemes of flat, generally pink flowers with double nectar spurs on the back.

CULTIVATION Mostly frost hardy, they prefer full sun, with afternoon shade in hot areas; they dislike humidity. A fertile, moist but well-drained soil and regular summer watering are vital. Pinch out tips to promote bushiness and cut back old stems after flowering. In the fall (autumn), propagate from seed or take cuttings to overwinter in a cool greenhouse.

Diascia rigescens

A vigorous trailing form with dense 6–8 in (15–20 cm) spikes of pink flowers at the upturned ends of each stem. Clumps may be 24 in (60 cm) across. Remove faded flower spikes and it will bloom all summer.

ZONES 8–10.

DICENTRA

Bleeding heart

Admired for their feathery leaves and the graceful carriage of their flowers, these plants do best in

Dicentra spectabilis

cool temperate or cold climates; they need the winter chill. The 20 species in this genus of annuals and perennials are natives of woodland and mountainous areas in Asia and North America. The pendent and heart-shaped flowers—in red, pink, white, purple and yellow—appear from mid-spring to early summer, though potted plants can be gently forced into early spring bloom if taken into a mildly warmed greenhouse at mid-winter.

CULTIVATION Mostly quite frost hardy, dicentras love humus-rich, moist but well-drained soil and some light shade. Propagate from seed in fall (autumn) or by division in late winter.

Dicentra spectabilis
Bleeding heart, Dutchman's breeches, lyre flower

Pink and white heart-shaped flowers on long arching stems appear in late spring and summer. After flowering, the foliage usually dies down to ground level. This perennial grows 24–36 in (60–90 cm) tall, with a spread of 18–24 in (45–60 cm). **'Alba'** is a pure white form with green-yellow markings and pale green leaves that will grow true from seed.

ZONES 2–9.

DIGITALIS
Foxglove

The medicinal properties of digitalis have been recognized since ancient times, and these plants are still used in the treatment of heart ailments. Natives of Europe, northern Africa and western Asia, these 22 species of biennials and perennials, some of them evergreen, are grown for their tall spikes of tubular, 2-lipped flowers which come in many colors: magenta, purple, white, cream, yellow, pink and lavender. The leaves are simple, mid-green and entire or toothed.

CULTIVATION They do best in cool climates and in partly-shaded, sheltered sites with humus-rich, well-drained soil. They vary from marginally frost hardy to fully frost hardy. Cut spent spikes down to the ground after spring flowering to encourage secondary spikes. Propagate from seed in fall

Useful Tip

Contact with the foliage of dicentras may exacerbate skin allergies, and ingestion of any part of the plant will cause mild stomach upset.

(autumn) or by division; they self-seed readily.

Digitalis purpurea
Common foxglove

This short-lived, frost-hardy erect perennial achieves a height of 3-5 ft (1–1.5 m) and a spread of 24 in (60 cm). The flowers may be purple, pink, rosy magenta, white or pale yellow, held above a rosette of rough, oval, deep green leaves. All parts of the plant, especially the leaves, are poisonous. Many seedling strains are available, grown as bedding annuals, the **Excelsior Hybrids** in mixed colors being very popular. *Digitalis purpurea* f. *albiflora* has pure white flowers sometimes lightly spotted brown inside; it will usually come true from seed, especially if it is isolated from other forms.

ZONES 5–10.

Useful Tip

Digitalis is poisonous.

Digitalis purpurea

EF

ECHINACEA

Coneflower

The 9 coneflower species, all native to the USA, share their common name with close relatives, the rudbeckias. They are clumping plants with thick edible roots. The daisy-like flowerheads are usually mauve-pink or purple, with darker and paler garden forms available. The dried roots and rhizomes of two species used in herbal medicine are said to enhance the body's resistance to infection.

CULTIVATION Very frost hardy, these plants like full sun and fertile soil. They dislike being disturbed, so divide them only to increase stock, otherwise leave them alone and mulch each spring. Deadhead regularly to prolong flowering.

Propagate by division or from root cuttings from winter to early spring.

Echinacea purpurea
syn. *Rudbeckia purpurea*
Purple coneflower

This showy, summer-flowering erect perennial has dark green, lance-shaped leaves and large, daisy-like, rosy purple flowers

Useful Tip

Place fresh cut flowers in a position indoors where they will get lots of light, but not direct sunlight.

Echinacea purpurea 'Robert Bloom'

with high, orange-brown central cones. The flowerheads, about 4 in (10 cm) wide, are borne singly on strong stems and are useful for cutting. It grows to 4 ft (1.2 m) and spreads about 18 in (45 cm). **'Robert Bloom'** has dark pink flowers, **'White Swan'** has pure white flowers; both have orange-brown centers.

ZONES 3–10.

ECHINOPS

Globe thistle

This genus, related to thistles, contains about 120 species of erect perennials, biennials and annuals native to southern Europe, central Asia, and the mountainous areas of tropical Africa. The cultivated species, which can reach 4 ft (1.2 m) or more, are an asset to the wild garden or herbaceous border and are good for fresh or dried flower arrangements. The foliage is usually gray-green and thistle-like though usually not as spiny. The ball-shaped flowerheads can be blue, blue-gray or white, the rich blues being the most favored, and up to 2 in (5 cm) in diameter.

CULTIVATION Both fully frost hardy and heat tolerant, these undemanding plants require nothing more than a sunny aspect and a well-drained soil of any quality. Cut them back to ground level in fall (autumn) or early winter. Propagate by division or from seed.

Echinops ritro

Echinops ritro

This perennial is a useful plant for the herbaceous border, and its globe-like, spiky flowers can be cut and dried for winter decoration. It has large, deeply cut, prickly leaves with downy undersides, silvery white stems and round, thistle-like, purplish-blue flowerheads in summer. Of upright habit, it grows 30 in (75 cm) tall and wide.

ZONES 3–10.

ERIGERON

Fleabane

Its common name referring to the alleged ability of some of its 200 species to repel fleas, this genus of annuals, biennials and perennials, some evergreen, occurs widely in temperate regions across the world, mostly in North America. The mainly erect stems are topped by masses of pink, white or blue, daisy-like flowers and are excellent subjects for a rock garden or the front of a border. Flowering occurs between late spring and mid-summer. 'Wayne Roderick' is one of many garden forms.

CULTIVATION Frost hardy, they prefer a sunny position sheltered from strong winds and moderately fertile, well-drained soil. Do not let them dry out during the growing season. Cut back immediately after flowering to encourage compact growth and prevent unwanted self-seeding. Some erigerons can become invasive. Propagate from seed or by division in spring. Divide every 2-3 years in late spring, and discard the woody crown.

Erigeron aureus

The wild forms of this species are short-lived perennials from the mountains of western North America. The selected form 'Canary Bird' is much longer-lived and reaches 4 in (10 cm) when in flower. The soft to bright yellow flowers are borne singly on stems above spoon-shaped, hairy, gray-green leaves.

ZONES 5–9.

Erigeron aureus 'Canary Bird'

ERYNGIUM

Sea holly, eryngo

These 230 species of biennials and perennials are relatives of the carrot. Mostly native to South America and Europe, they are grown for their distinctive foliage and spiny, collared flowerheads, which usually have a bluish metallic sheen. They flower over a long period in summer and may be dried for winter decoration. The common name 'holly' arises from the spiny margins of the strongly colored, thistle-like bracts, which surround the central flower.

A number of named hybrids are available including the rather striking 'Jos Eijking'.

CULTIVATION Mostly frost hardy, they need sun, good drainage and sandy soil. Plants tend to collapse in wet, heavy

Useful Tip

 Fresh manure applied to the garden will burn your plants; always use well-rotted manure, and make sure that it does not build up around the bases of plants and trees.

Eryngium amethystinum

ground in winter. Propagate species from fresh seed and selected forms by root cuttings in winter or by division in spring.

Eryngium amethystinum

This perennial comes from Italy and the Balkans. Its leaves are basal and up to 6 in (15 cm) long, spiny and mid-green. The ovoid flowerheads are the color of amethysts, surrounded by silvery-blue bracts about 2 in (5 cm) long, and are produced on silvery blue stems. Plants may reach 30 in (75 cm) in height.

ZONES 7–10.

ERYSIMUM

syn. *Cheiranthus*
Wallflower

This genus, now including *Cheiranthus*, consists of 80 species of annuals and perennials from Europe to central Asia, with a smaller number in North America. Some, such as the hybrid **'Orange Flame'**, are ideal for rock gardens; others suit a border setting. Short-lived species are best grown as biennials. Some form woody bases and become leggy after a few years; they should be replaced with younger specimens. Some are winter to spring-flowering plants, while others, grown in mild climates, will flower all winter or all year

Eryngium 'Jos Eijking'

Erysimum 'Moonlight'

round. Older types have a sweet fragrance; newer cultivars, although unscented, flower well over a long season.

CULTIVATION Mostly frost hardy, they do best in well-drained, fertile soil in an open, sunny position. Trim perennials lightly after flowering to prevent them becoming leggy. Propagate from seed in spring or cuttings in summer.

Erysimum 'Moonlight'

A mat-forming, evergreen perennial with inversely lanceolate leaves, it grows 10 in (25 cm) tall and about 18 in (45 cm) wide. It flowers from early spring well into summer and produces short racemes of cheerful sulfur-yellow flowers. It makes a most attractive rock garden plant or subject for the front of a border.

ZONES 6–9.

EUPHORBIA

Milkweed, spurge

Close to 2000 species belong in this genus, among them annuals, biennials, perennials, subshrubs, trees, and numerous succulent species which bear a remarkable resemblance to cacti. Most are tropical and subtropical, though there are

Euphorbia griffithii 'Fireglow'

Useful Tip

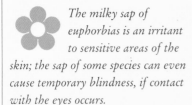

The milky sap of euphorbias is an irritant to sensitive areas of the skin; the sap of some species can even cause temporary blindness, if contact with the eyes occurs.

many temperate species. Despite the great variety of forms, the flowers of all species are almost identical: very much reduced, consisting of only a stigma and a stamen, always green, and usually carried in small clusters. Species with showy bracts are the most widely grown.

CULTIVATION Thriving in sun or part-shade in moist, well-drained soil, they vary from frost hardy to tender, depending on the species; the succulent species tend to be frost tender. Propagate from cuttings in spring or summer, allowing succulent species to dry and callus before placing in barely-damp sand, by division in early spring or fall (autumn), or from seed in fall (autumn) or spring.

Euphorbia griffithii

This perennial from the eastern Himalayas, which grows to a height of 3 ft (1 m), produces

Euphorbia griffithii

small, yellow flowers surrounded by brilliant orange-red bracts in summer. The lanceolate, green leaves have prominent pinkish midribs and turn red and yellow in fall (autumn). **'Fireglow'** is at its best in early summer.

ZONES 6–9.

FELICIA

Blue daisy

Named after Herr Felix, mayor of Regensburg on the Danube in the mid-nineteenth century, this genus from southern Africa to Arabia consists of 80 species of annuals, perennials and evergreen sub-shrubs. These sprawling, mound-forming plants with aromatic foliage are grown for their masses of daisy-like flowers (blue, with yellow disc florets). In mild climates, they flower on and off all year round.

CULTIVATION Fully frost hardy to frost tender, preferring full sun and well-drained, humus-rich, gravely soil, they are intolerant of wet conditions. In winter, protect frost-tender perennials with open-ended cloches in all but the mildest climates. Deadhead regularly to prolong the flowering season, pinch off young shoots to promote bushiness, and prune straggly shoots. Take cuttings in late summer or fall (autumn) or sow seed in the spring.

Felicia fruticosa

Felicia fruticosa
syns *Aster fruticosus,*
Diplopappus fruticosus

This is a bushy perennial 2–4 ft (0.6–1.2 m) high with tiny heath-like, linear leaves and pink, white or purple flowerheads in spring and early summer. The flowering period is long and extremely abundant. Cut back after flowering to encourage compact growth and a good crop of flowers the following year.

ZONES 9–11.

FILIPENDULA

The 10 species of herbaceous perennials in this genus grow wild in northern temperate regions; all occur naturally in moist waterside habitats, apart from *Filipendula vulgaris*, which grows on dry, chalky grassland. Their erect stems bear alternate pinnate leaves and, from late spring to late summer, large plumes of tiny red, pink or white, 5-petalled flowers with fluffy stamens. They do well in a

Filipendula purpurea 'Elegans'

woodland garden, at the back of borders and in waterside positions.

CULTIVATION Grow these fully frost-hardy plants in full sun or part-shade in any moisture-retentive but well-drained soil. Some species will even thrive in swampy, boggy sites. Propagate from seed or by division in spring or fall (autumn). Watch for powdery mildew.

Filipendula purpurea
Japanese meadowsweet

A native of Japan, this clump-forming perennial reaches a height of 4 ft (1.2 m) with deeply divided, toothed leaves. In summer it bears large terminal heads composed of masses of tiny crimson-purple flowers. This is a beautiful plant for growing near a water feature. **'Elegans'** has light greenish yellow foliage.

ZONES 6–9.

Useful Tip

Choose a shady site for Filipendula purpurea *'Elegans' to maintain the golden coloration of its leaves at its best.*

Filipendula ulmaria 'Variegata'

GH

GAURA

The genus name for these 20 species of annuals, biennials, perennials and subshrubs means 'gorgeous'. They grow wild in moist places and prairies of North America and have a tendency to be weedy, despite their showy flowers. They have simple, narrow leaves and clusters of flat, star-shaped, pink or white flowers. The evening primrose (*Oenothera*) is a relative. They are very successful as border plants.

CULTIVATION Trouble-free gauras grow well in full sun and light, well-drained soil. After flowering, cut them ruthlessly to ground level. Propagate from seed in fall (autumn) or spring, by division in spring, or from cuttings in summer.

Gaura lindheimeri

Native to the USA–Mexico border region, this clump-forming, long-flowering perennial is useful for backgrounds and mixed flower borders. Its loosely branched stems are covered with tiny hairs and its leaves are spoon- to lance-shaped. From spring to fall (autumn), it produces long panicles of pinkish buds which open at dawn to white flowers. It grows 4 ft (1.2 m) tall and 3 ft (1 m) across.

ZONES 5–10.

Gaura lindheimeri

GAZANIA

Theodore of Gaza (1398–1478) was a medieval scholar whose name was given to this genus from tropical and southern Africa, consisting of about 16 species of low-growing annuals and perennials. They are grown for their colorful, even gaudy flowers. The leaves are entire or deeply lobed, long and narrow, often dark green on top and white- or silver-gray-felted beneath; some species have silvery hairs on both sides. Flowers appear from early spring until summer. Single flowerheads, borne on short stalks, come in a range of colors and intermediate shades: cream, yellow, gold, pink, red, buff and brown, usually with contrasting bands or spots at the petal bases. Most modern varieties are hybrids from several South African species; they are marginally frost hardy and useful in coastal gardens for bedding, rock gardens, pots and tubs, and for

Useful Tip

Most gazanias can withstand short periods below freezing, but if you choose to overwinter them under glass, watch for gray mold (Botrytis) and aphids.

Gazania 'Gwen's Pink'

Gazania hybrid

binding soil on slopes. **'Gwen's Pink'** is one of several popular cultivars; others include **'Flore Pleno'** (double yellow flower) and **'Double Orange'** (orange flower with a double center).

CULTIVATION They thrive in full sun in sandy, fairly dry, well-drained soil. Mulch with compost and water during dry periods. Propagate by division or from cuttings in fall (autumn), or from seed in late winter to early spring.

GENTIANA

Gentian

Growing wild mostly in alpine meadows and occasionally in woodlands, the some 400 species of this genus include annuals, biennials and perennials; some are evergreen. Flowers are often trumpet-shaped and while deep or sky blues are the usual flower colors, white, cream, yellow and even red are seen. Flowering takes place from spring to fall (autumn). Gentians are useful in rock gardens and sloping hillside gardens.

CULTIVATION They grow well in cooler regions and like well-drained, moisture-retentive soil rich in humus; some will even grow naturally in limestone soil. Plant in either sun or semi-shade. Propagate by division in spring or from fresh seed in fall (autumn). Divide fall (autumn)-flowering species every 3 years in early spring, planting out in fresh soil.

Gentiana asclepiadea
Willow gentian

The arching stems of this loose clump-forming perennial bear slender, willow-like leaves. In early fall (autumn) many rich violet-blue flowers appear in the leaf axils on the upper stems. Clumps can reach 3 ft (1 m) in height and 24 in (60 cm) across.

ZONES 6–9.

Gentiana asclepiadea

GERANIUM

Cranesbill

Geraniums grow all over the world, mainly in cool-temperate regions. More than 300 species of clump-forming annuals, biennials and perennials exist, some of them evergreen. Named 'cranesbill' for the shape of their small, dry fruitlets, geraniums are often confused with the genus *Pelargonium*, also commonly and inaccurately known as 'geraniums'. Unlike pelargonium flowers, which are irregularly shaped or marked, geranium flowers are symmetrical; they have 5 petals and are pink to blue or purple and white. Held on long stalks, their broadly circular, often palmately-lobed leaves may be textured, colored or marked and are often aromatic. With their attractive flowers they are useful for rock gardens, ground covers and borders, and compact species are ideal for containers.

CULTIVATION Mostly quite frost hardy, they prefer a sunny site and damp, well-drained soil. Transplant during winter. Propagate from cuttings in summer or seed in spring, or by division in fall (autumn).

Geranium x oxonianum

This vigorous upright hybrid of *Geranium endressi* and *G. versicolor* forms clumps up to 30 in (75 cm) high. It has light green, wrinkled leaves with conspicuous veining and trumpet-shaped flushed pink flowers with darker veins. The flowering period is from late spring to mid-fall (mid-autumn). Cultivars include **'Wargrave Pink'** and **'Claridge Druce'**.

ZONES 5–9.

Geranium x *oxonianum* 'Wargrave Pink'

GERBERA

Linnaeus named this genus of around 40 perennial species from Africa, Madagascar and Asia to honor a German colleague by the name of Traugott Gerber. The showy flowerheads, in almost every color except blue and purple, are carried on bare stems 18 in (45 cm) long. They are ideal rockery plants in frost-free climates. Only one species, *Gerbera jamesonii*, is commonly cultivated, along with its numerous hybrids.

CULTIVATION They need full sun to part-shade in hot areas, and fertile, well-drained soil. Water well during summer. Gerberas make good greenhouse plants, where they require good light and regular feeding during the growing season. Propagate from seed in fall (autumn) or early spring, from cuttings in summer or by division from late winter to early spring.

Gerbera jamesonii cultivars

orange or red, in spring or summer. Flowers are 3 in (8 cm) across. Florists' gerberas derive from crosses between *Gerbera jamesonii* and the tropical *G. viridifolia*. Some achieve flowerheads as much as 12 in (30 cm) in diameter; others feature a wide range of colors, as well as double and quilled forms.

Gerbera jamesonii
Barberton daisy,
Transvaal daisy

Native to South Africa, this is one of the most decorative of all daisies and is an excellent cut flower. Long stems rise from a basal rosette of deeply lobed, lance-shaped leaves, bearing single flowers in white, pink, yellow,

ZONES 8–11.

Useful Tip

 Count the stamen rings in the center of florists' gerberas if you want to avoid buying blooms which are past their prime: there should be no more than three.

GEUM

Avens

Equally at home in the temperate and cooler zones of the northern and southern hemispheres, this genus of 50 or so herbaceous perennials is useful in a rock garden or at the front of a border. Basal rosettes of hairy, lobed leaves contrast with masses of red, orange and yellow flowers with prominent stamens. Flowering is from late spring until early fall (autumn), and almost all year in frost-free areas.

CULTIVATION Frost hardy, they prefer a sunny, open position and moist, well-drained soil. Propagate from seed or by division in fall (autumn) or spring.

Geum chiloense
syns *Geum coccineum* of gardens, *G. quellyon*
Scarlet avens

This Chilean native is a good border plant, achieving a height of 24 in (60 cm) and a spread of 12 in (30 cm). It forms a basal rosette of deep green, pinnate leaves to 12 in (30 cm) long. The vivid scarlet, cup-shaped flowers appear in terminal panicles in summer. **'Lady Stratheden'** (syn. 'Goldball') has semi-double, golden yellow flowers. **'Mrs Bradshaw'** bears rounded, semi-double, scarlet flowers.

ZONES 5–9.

Geum chiloense 'Lady Stratheden'

HELENIUM

Sneezeweed, Helen's flower

Striking in a flower arrangement as in a garden border, these 40 species of annual, biennial and perennial herbs grow wild in the Americas. The mid-green leaves are oval to lanceolate and alternate on erect stems. The daisy-like flowerheads appear in summer and have yellow, red-brown or orange ray florets and yellow, yellow-green, red or brown disc florets.

CULTIVATION Easy to grow in any temperate climate as long as they get sun, they are frost hardy. They prefer moist and well-drained soil. Remove spent flowers regularly to prolong the flowering period. Propagate by division of old clumps in winter or from seed in spring or fall (autumn).

Helenium autumnale
Common sneezeweed

This North America perennial grows about 5 ft (1.5 m) tall and flowers from late summer to mid-fall (mid-autumn). Several garden forms derive from this species, their flowers ranging from yellow to maroon, as well as blends of yellow and russet tones.

ZONES 3–9.

Helenium autumnale

HELIANTHEMUM

Rock rose, sun rose

Helianthemum means 'flower of sunshine', an appropriate name for flowers that only open in bright sunlight. More than 100 species grow wild on rocky and scrubby ground in temperate zones around the world. Sun roses are sturdy, short-lived, evergreen or semi-evergreen shrubs or subshrubs. Their bushy foliage ranges in colour from silver to mid-green. There are many garden forms, mostly of low, spreading habit. Wild plants have flowers 1 in (25 mm) across, which resemble wild roses; garden forms range from white through yellow and salmon-pink to red and orange, and even some double flowers.

CULTIVATION Plant in full sun in freely-draining, coarse soil, to which a little peat or compost is added during dry periods. Cut back lightly after flowering to encourage a second flush in fall (autumn). Propagate from seed or cuttings.

Helianthemum nummularium

A neat, prostrate habit characterizes this variable species from Europe and Turkey. Its small, profuse flowers vary in color from yellow or cream to pink and orange. Most cultivars traditionally listed under this name are in fact of hybrid origin.

ZONES 5–10.

HELIANTHUS

This genus of the daisy family comprises around 70 species of annuals and perennials, all native to the Americas. It includes many ornamentals, as well as plants used for livestock fodder, the Jerusalem

Helianthemum nummularium

Helianthus x *multiflorus* 'Loddon Gold'

artichoke with edible tubers and one of the world's most important oilseed plants. The leaves are hairy, often sticky and the stems are tall and rough. Large, daisy-like, usually golden-yellow flowerheads are on prolonged display from summer to fall (autumn).

CULTIVATION Frost hardy, they prefer full sun, shelter from wind and a well-drained soil. Fertilize in spring to promote large blooms and water generously in dry conditions. After flowering, cut perennial species down to the base. Propagate from seed or by division in fall (autumn) or early spring.

Helianthus x *multiflorus*

This hybrid is a clump-forming perennial which reaches 6 ft (1.8 m) in height and 3 ft (1 m) across. The domed flowers, appearing in late summer and mid-fall (mid-autumn), can be up to 6 in (15 cm) across. The most popular cultivars include 'Capenoch Star', 'Loddon Gold', 'Soleil d'Or' and 'Triomphe de Gand'.

ZONES 5–9.

HELIOPSIS

Orange sunflower, ox eye

The name *Heliopsis* means 'like a sunflower' and these North American prairie perennials do resemble sunflowers, though on a rather reduced and more manageable scale. There are about 12 species. The stems are stiff and branching and the leaves are toothed and mid- to dark green. The solitary, usually yellow flowers are up to 3in (8 cm) in diameter and make flamboyant cut flowers.

CULTIVATION Although very frost hardy and easy to grow even in poor conditions, they do best in a sunny position in fertile, moist

Heliopsis helianthoides 'Light of Loddon'

but well-drained soil. Deadhead regularly to prolong the flower display and cut back to ground level after flowers fade. Propagate from seed or cuttings in spring, or by division in spring or fall (autumn).

Heliopsis helianthoides

This species grows to 5 ft (1.5 m) tall and 3 ft (1 m) in spread. It has coarse, hairy leaves and golden yellow flowers in summer. **'Light of Loddon'** has rough, hairy leaves and strong stems that carry dahlia-like, bright yellow, double flowers in late summer. It grows to a height of 3 ft (1 m) and a spread of 24 in (60 cm). **'Patula'** has semi-double orange flowers.

ZONES 4–9.

HELLEBORUS

Hellebore

These 15 species of winter- and spring-flowering perennials and evergreens are native to cooler regions of Europe and western Asia. They bear beautiful, open flowers in white or shades of green, red and purple and are effective planted in drifts or massed in the shade of deciduous trees. All hellebores are poisonous.

CULTIVATION Grow in part-shade and moist, well-drained, humus-rich soil. Do not allow the soil to dry out in summer. Cut off old leaves from deciduous species just as the buds start to appear. Remove flowerheads after seeds

Helleborus argutifolius

drop. A top-dressing of compost or manure after flowering is of benefit. Propagate from seed or by division in fall (autumn) or early spring. Check for aphids.

Helleborus argutifolius
syns *Helleborus corsicus,*
H. lividus subsp. *corsicus*
Corsican hellebore

This robust evergreen blooms in late winter and early spring, making it one of the earliest-flowering hellebores. It is also the most tolerant of sun and the most resistant to drought. Large clusters of cup-shaped, green flowers, about 2 in (5 cm) across, are borne on an upright spike above divided, spiny-margined, deep green foliage. It has a clump-forming habit, reaching 24 in (60 cm) in height and 24-36 in (60–90 cm) in width. Grow in neutral to alkaline soil in full sun or dappled shade.

ZONES 6–9.

Useful Tip

There is almost literally a daylily hybrid for every day of the year, and even some for the nights! Nocturnal daylilies open in the late afternoon and last through the night.

HEMEROCALLIS
Daylily

These temperate east Asian perennials, some of them semi- or fully evergreen, are well loved for their showy, often fragrant flowers that come in a vibrant range of colors. Individual blooms last only for a day, hence *Hemerocallis*, meaning 'beautiful for a day', but are borne in great numbers on strong stems above tall, grassy foliage and continue to flower from early summer to fall (autumn). The flower size varies from 3 in (8 cm) miniatures to giants of 6 in (15 cm) or more; they may be single or double. The plants vary in height from about 24 in (60 cm) to 3 ft (1 m). Plant in an herbaceous border among shrubs or naturalize in grassy woodland areas.

CULTIVATION Choose the site with care, as the flowers turn their heads towards the sun. Most are

Hemerocallis Hybrid 'Stella d'Oro'

fully hardy, and while they prefer sun, will grow well—and give brighter colors—in part-shade. They need a reasonably good soil that does not dry out. Propagate by division in fall (autumn) or spring, and divide clumps every 3 or 4 years. Seed-raised cultivars do not come true to type. Check for slugs and snails in early spring, and also for aphids or spider mites.

Hemerocallis Hybrids

There is a vast number of modern hybrids, and almost all the cultivated species of *Hemerocallis* have played their part. Most are grown for the size and texture of blooms and their rich or delicate coloring, often with an 'eye' of contrasting color in the center; others are grown more for the massed effect of smaller or more delicate, spidery flowers. 'So Excited' is a popular hybrid and 'Stella d'Oro' is one of a new range of miniatures.

ZONES 5–11.

HESPERIS

From the Mediterranean and temperate Asia, this genus consists of 60 species of biennials and herbaceous perennials allied to stocks (*Matthiola*). They have narrow, usually undivided leaves that may be toothed or toothless, and showy pink, purple or white flowers in long racemes. Some species bear

Hesperis matronalis, white form

scented flowers. They are especially suited to a border or wild garden.

CULTIVATION Frost hardy, they thrive in full sun and moist but well-drained, neutral to alkaline, not too fertile soil. The species are readily grown in temperate areas and will naturalize, but cultivars are sometimes more reluctant. Propagate from seed or cuttings and check regularly for mildew and also for attack from slugs and snails.

Hesperis matronalis
Dame's rocket, sweet rocket

Grown for its flowers which become very fragrant on humid evenings, this species grows wild from Europe to central Asia. It has smooth, narrowly-oval leaves and branching flowerheads with white to lilac flowers borne in summer. Of erect habit, it reaches 12–36 in (30–90 cm) in height with a spread of about 24 in (60 cm). Plants lose their vigor after a time and are best renewed every 2 to 3 years.

ZONES 3–9.

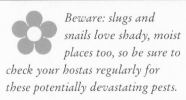

Useful Tip

Beware: slugs and snails love shady, moist places too, so be sure to check your hostas regularly for these potentially devastating pests.

HOSTA
Plantain lily

This genus of 40 easily grown, frost-hardy perennials valued for their decorative foliage originates from Japan and China. All produce wide, handsome leaves: some marbled or marked with white, others with bluish-green. All-yellow foliage forms are also available. They do well in large pots or planters, are excellent for ground cover and add an exotic touch planted on the margins of lily ponds or in bog gardens. Stems about 18 in (45 cm) tall bear nodding, white, pink or shades of purple and blue, bell- or trumpet-shaped flowers during warmer weather. Both the leaves and the flowers are popular for floral arrangements.

Hosta plantaginea

CULTIVATION They do well in shade and rich, moist, neutral, well-drained soil. Feed regularly during the growing season. Propagate by division in early spring and guard against snails and slugs.

Hosta plantaginea
August lily, fragrant plantain lily

Popular for its pure white, fragrant flowers on 30 in (75 cm) stems, this species has mid-green leaves forming a mound 3 ft (1 m) across. It flowers in late summer.

ZONES 3–10.

HYPERICUM

St John's wort

This large and varied genus has representatives worldwide across a broad range of habitats. It includes some 400 species of annuals, perennials, shrubs and a few small trees, some of them evergreen but mostly deciduous. They are popular for their showy flowers in shades of yellow with a central mass of prominent golden stamens. Species range in size from tiny perennials good for rockeries, to those over 10 ft (3 m) tall.

CULTIVATION Mostly cool-climate plants, they prefer full sun but will tolerate some shade. They do best in fertile, well-drained soil, with plentiful water in late spring and summer. Remove seed capsules after flowering and prune in winter to maintain a rounded shape. Cultivars are propagated from cuttings in summer, and species from seed in fall (autumn) or from cuttings in summer. Some species are susceptible to rust.

Hypericum cerastoides
syn. *Hypericum rhodoppeum*

A dense mound-forming perennial with oval, gray-green leaves and clusters of bright yellow, cup-shaped flowers borne in late spring and early summer. It has an upright, slightly spreading habit and grows to 12 in (30 cm) tall and 18 in (45 cm) across. It is frost hardy, and is a colorful asset in rock gardens.

ZONES 6–9.

Hypericum cerastoides

IKL

IBERIS

The 50 species of this genus are grown for their decorative effect in borders, bedding and rock gardens. These annuals, perennials and evergreen subshrubs are mainly from southern Europe, northern Africa and western Asia. The showy flowers are borne either as flattish heads in colors of white, red and purple, or in erect racemes of pure white.

CULTIVATION Fully to marginally frost hardy, they require a warm, sunny position and a well-drained, light soil, preferably with added lime or dolomite. Propagate from seed in spring or fall (autumn) or cuttings in summer. They may self-sow, but are unlikely to become invasive.

Iberis sempervirens
Candytuft, evergreen candytuft

This frost-hardy species from southern Europe is a low, spreading perennial which makes an attractive addition to a rock garden. It grows only 6-12 in (15–30 cm) high and 18-24 in (45–60 cm) across. It has narrow, dark green leaves and bears dense, rounded heads of unscented white flowers in spring and early summer. Trim candytufts back lightly after flowering. The glossy, dark green leaves and semi-spherical white flowers of 'Snowflake' make it a popular cultivar.

ZONES 4–11.

Iberis sempervirens

IRIS

Appropriately named after the Greek goddess of the rainbow, the beautiful flowers of this genus, which has more than 200 species native to the northern hemisphere temperate zones, come in a wide range of colors. The distinctive flowers have 6 petals: 3 outer petals, called 'falls', which droop away from the center and alternate with the inner petals, called 'standards'. There are many hybrids. Irises are divided into 2 main groups: **rhizomatous** and **bulbous**.

Rhizomatous irises have sword-shaped leaves, are sometimes evergreen, and are subdivided into 3 groups: **bearded** (or flag) irises, with a tuft of hairs (the 'beard') on the 3 lower petals; **beardless** irises, without the tuft; and **crested** or **Evansia** irises, with a raised crest instead of a beard. There are numerous species and hybrids of bearded irises and these are further subdivided into Tall, Intermediate and Dwarf classes, the most popular being the Tall Bearded iris, which has many cultivars. Among beardless irises, several species and hybrids exist, most notable being the North American **Louisiana** irises and their hybrids, the East Asian **Laevigatae** or **Water** irises, the North American **Pacific Coast** irises and hybrids and the Eurasian **Spuria** and **Siberian** irises and hybrids.

There are 3 groups of bulbous irises: the difficult **Juno** and **Reticulata** irises from Asia, and the easier **Xiphium** irises from the Mediterranean, the so-called **English**, **Spanish** and **Dutch** hybrids of which are commonly sold as cut flowers.

CULTIVATION Growing conditions vary greatly, but in general rhizomatous irises, apart from

Iris, Louisiana Hybrid

Iris, Louisiana Hybrid, 'Vermilion Treasure'

crested irises, are very frost hardy and prefer a sunny position. Some beardless types like very moist soil. Bulbous irises are very frost hardy and prefer a sunny position with ample moisture during growth, but very little during their summer dormancy. Bulbous irises should be planted in fall (autumn) and are prone to virus infection and so need to be kept free of aphids, which will spread the infection. Propagate irises by division in late summer after flowering or from seed in fall (autumn). Named cultivars should only be divided.

Iris, Louisiana Hybrids

An increasingly popular, colorful group of evergreen, beardless hybrids with fine, strap-like foliage. Basically swamp or water irises, but will do well in the garden if watered well; they do best in a sunny position with average to damp, humus-rich garden soil; they are not fully frost hardy. They form substantial clumps and need to be divided after 2-3 years. Plants rarely exceed 3 ft (1 m) in height and are usually much shorter. Hybrids include 'Art World', 'Bluebonnet Sue', 'Exclusive Label', 'Guessing Game', 'Insider' and 'Vermilion Treasure'.

ZONES 7–10.

KNIPHOFIA

Red-hot poker, torch lily, tritoma

The common name 'red-hot poker' dates back to the days of the coal fire and describes the original colors most often seen before plant breeders such as Max Leichtlin (1831–1910) began developing new species; today, flowers can also be pink, orange and yellow. The 68 species of perennials, some of which are evergreen, are native to southern and eastern Africa. They are upright, tufted plants with long leaves and showy, tubular flowers in dense spikes on tall bare stems; summer flowering is most common, but some cultivars flower in winter and early spring. Sizes vary from head-high to miniature types,

Kniphofia x *praecox* cultivar

no more than 24 in (60 cm) tall, and they attract bees and nectar-feeding birds.

CULTIVATION Frost hardy to somewhat frost tender, they like an open position in full sun, well-drained soil and plenty of water in summer. They will tolerate wind and coastal conditions. In areas with winter temperatures below 5°F (–15°C), they can be carefully lifted and stored indoors to be planted again in spring, although heavy mulching is preferable. From spring onwards, fertilize monthly. Remove dead flower stems and leaves in late fall (autumn). Propagate species from seed or by division in spring; cultivars by division in spring.

Kniphofia x *praecox*
Red-hot poker

This South African species is the most common in the wild and reaches up to 5 ft (1.5 m) when in bloom. Its slender leaves, up to 24 in (60 cm) long, are heavily keeled and serrated. Vivid red or yellow flowers appear in early summer. It thrives in full sun and is tolerant of long dry periods.

ZONES 7–10.

LEUCANTHEMUM

This genus, comprising about 25 species of annuals and perennials from Europe and temperate Asia, was previously included in

Leucanthemum x *superbum*

Chrysanthemum by many botanists. They are clump-forming plants with variably toothed or lobed leaves and long-stalked, daisy-like flowerheads arising from leafy stems. Flowers have white or yellow ray florets and yellow disc florets. While mostly vigorous, adaptable plants, some fail to thrive in warmer climates.

CULTIVATION Largely undemanding, these plants grow well in a perennial border or garden bed in full sun or morning shade in moderately fertile, moist but well-drained soil. Propagate from seed, cuttings or by division.

Leucanthemum x *superbum*
syns *Chrysanthemum maximum* of gardens, *C.* x *superbum*
Shasta daisy

This robust perennial was first noticed naturalized on the slopes of Mount Shasta in Washington State, USA and attracted the attention of the famous plant breeder Luther Burbank. Plants reach a height and spread of 2-3 ft (60–90 cm). Large, daisy-like, white flowerheads with pale golden centers may be 3 in (8 cm) across and are carried high above the dark, shiny, toothed leaves in summer and early fall (autumn). They are believed to be hybrids between

Leucanthemum maximum and *L. lacustre*. Many cultivars, always white-flowered, exist, including doubles as well as singles, some with fringed petals.

ZONES 5–10.

LIATRIS
Blazing star

Relatives of the daisy, although bearing no visible resemblance in terms of flowers or foliage, these 40 species of perennials come from the central and eastern regions of North America. In summer they sprout tall, cylindrical spikes of fluffy flowers, crowded with small flowerheads opening from the top

Liatris spicata

downward and they have distinctive corm- or tuber-like, swollen, flattened stems. They make excellent border plants.

CULTIVATION Thriving on minimum care, they grow in most soils and conditions including damp places such as stream banks and ditches; they do best, however, in climates with low humidity. Propagation is from seed or by division of old clumps in winter.

Liatris spicata
syn. *Liatris callilepis* of gardens
Gay feather, spike gay feather

This low-growing species is grown for cut flowers and it attracts bees and butterflies. The late summer flowers are lilac-purple, although they can occur in pink and white. The fluffy flower spikes look like feather dusters

and open from the top down wards, which is the opposite of most flower spikes. It grows to a height of 24 in (60 cm), with thickened, corm-like rootstocks and basal tufts of grassy, mid-green foliage. Cultivars include **'Floristan Violett'** and **'Floristan Weiss'**, both up to 5 ft (1.5 m) tall, and **'Kobold'**, a dwarf type.

ZONES 3–10.

LIMONIUM

Statice, sea lavender

These are popular plants for seaside holiday homes because of their tolerance to sea spray and low rainfall. This genus of some 150 species is distributed among the world's temperate regions, mostly in saline coastal and desert environments, with major concentrations in the

Liatris spicata 'Kobold'

Limonium gmelinii

Mediterranean, central Asia and the Canary Islands. They include evergreen and deciduous sub-shrubs, perennials, biennials and annuals. The tapered, almost stalk-less leaves appear in basal rosettes. Some annuals are grown in borders for their many-colored heads of small, papery flowers which are good as cut and dried flowers.

CULTIVATION Statices are easi-ly grown in full sun and well-drained, sandy soil and they do well in coastal gardens. Lightly fer-tilize plants in spring, while the flowerheads are developing. Propagate by division in spring, from seed in early spring or fall (autumn) or from root cuttings in late winter. Transplant during win-ter or early spring.

Limonium gmelinii

This perennial from eastern Europe and Siberia grows to 24 in (60 cm) tall in any deep, well-drained soil in full sun. It pro-duces leaves in spikelets and bears lilac tubular flowers.

ZONES 4–10.

LOBELIA

This is a large genus of 370 species of annuals, perennials and shrubs from the temperate regions, partic-ularly of the Americas and Africa. Their habitats range from marshes to meadows, woodlands to deserts and even mountain slopes. All are grown for their attractive flowers, which are often very brightly

Lobelia x *gerardii*

colored, and their neat foliage. Their form varies from low bedding types to tall, herbaceous perennials or shrubs, and they make excellent edging, flower box, hanging basket and rock garden specimens. Some are suited to wild gardens or water's edge sites.

CULTIVATION These frost-hardy to somewhat frost-tender plants are best grown in well-drained, moist, light loam enriched with animal manure or compost. Most grow in sun or part-shade and prefer dry winter conditions. Fertilize weekly with a liquid manure during flowering, and encourage repeat flowering by pruning after the first flowers fade. Propagate annuals from seed in spring, perennial species from seed or by division in spring or fall (autumn), and perennial cultivars by division only. Transplant from late fall (autumn) until early spring.

Lobelia cardinalis
Cardinal flower

Named for its scarlet floral display which takes place in late summer to mid-fall (mid-autumn), this clump-forming perennial from eastern North America is useful for growing in wet places and beside streams and ponds. Spikes of brilliant, scarlet-red flowers are produced on branching stems above green or deep bronze-purple foliage. It achieves a height of 3 ft (1 m) and a spread of 12 in (30 cm).

ZONES 3–10.

Lobelia x gerardii

This robust perennial is a hybrid derived from *Lobelia cardinalis* and *L. siphilitica* that can grow as tall as 5 ft (1.5 m). It has pink, violet or purple flowers and makes a beautiful garden specimen. The well-known cultivar 'Vedrariensis' produces racemes of violet-blue flowers in late summer; it has dark green, lanceolate leaves. These hybrids prefer to grow in moist but well-drained soil in full sun.

ZONES 7–10.

Lobelia cardinalis

LUPINUS

Lupin, lupine

The plants in this legume genus are grown for their long, erect spikes of showy pea-flowers in a range of colors. They are also valued as 'green manure' (because of their good nitrogen-fixing properties), used for animal fodder, and a few species are even grown for grain, for consumption by both humans and livestock. The group includes 200 species of annuals, perennials, semi-evergreen and evergreen shrubs and subshrubs, mainly native to North America, southern Europe and North Africa. The compound leaves are distinct among legumes in being palmate, with 5 or more leaflets radiating from a common stalk, rather than the usual pinnate arrangement. Flowers may be blue, purple, pink, white, yellow, orange or red.

CULTIVATION Most prefer cool wet winters and long dry summers. They like plenty of water in the growing season and should be mulched in dry areas. Plant them in full sun and in well-drained, moderately fertile, slightly acidic, sandy soil. Remove spent flowers to prolong plant life and to prevent self-seeding. Propagate species from seed in fall (autumn).

Lupinus, Russell Hybrids

Lupinus, **Russell Hybrids**

Russell lupins were first named in 1937, after George Russell, a lupin enthusiast who over some years selected the best seedlings from open-pollinated plants of *Lupinus polyphyllus*, and then released a selection to great acclaim. These vigorous hybrids (the other major parent likely to be *L.hartwegii*) form a large clump of deeply divided, mid-green leaves, and bear long spikes of large, strongly-colored flowers in cream, pink, orange, blue or violet—even bicolored—in late spring and summer. They reach a height of 3 ft (1 m). '**Noble Maiden**', '**Polar Princess**' and '**Troop the Colour**' are popular; '**Lulu**' is a dwarf strain.

ZONES 3–9.

LYCHNIS

Campion, catchfly

Some of the 15-20 species in this genus have been grown for hundreds of years. They are related to *Silene*, the exact distinction being somewhat vague. Native to temperate regions of the northern hemisphere, these biennials and perennials are grown for their summer flowers of white through pinks and oranges to deep red. Petals in many species are notched or deeply forked, or even, in some, divided into narrow teeth.

CULTIVATION Easy to grow in cooler climates, these plants are frost hardy, but prefer a sunny site and well-drained soil. Trim spent stems after flowering and deadhead frequently to prolong the flower-

Lupinus, Russell Hybrid, 'Polar Princess'

Lychnis chalcedonica

ing season. Propagate by division or from seed in fall (autumn) or early spring. Some species self-seed readily.

Lychnis chalcedonica
Maltese cross

A favorite in gardens for well over 300 years, this perennial from far eastern Europe produces such a dazzling orange-red that you may be wise to choose companion plants with care. The shape of the flower gives it its common name. Plants reach about 4 ft (1.2 m) in height and flowers appear fairly briefly in early summer. White and pink varieties exist, as does one with double flowers, but these are uncommon.

ZONES 4–10.

Lychnis coronaria
Rose campion, dusty miller, mullein pink

In ancient times, the deep-rose pink to scarlet flowers of this striking species were used for garlands and crowns. A clump-forming perennial, sometimes grown as a biennial, it grows to a height of 30 in (75 cm) and spreads about 18 in (45 cm) wide. This low-maintenance plant is drought tolerant and often self-seeds. Silvery white, downy leaves and many-branched gray stems carry large flowers throughout summer. **'Alba'** is a white-flowered cultivar.

ZONES 4–10.

Lychnis coronaria

LYSIMACHIA

Loosestrife

The origin of the names (the botanical name being Latinized Greek for 'ending strife') is now unclear. The vast majority of the 150 species are found in China, the rest mainly in temperate and subtropical regions of the northern hemisphere; a few are found in Africa, Australia and South America. This genus of mainly evergreen perennials and shrubs of the primula family vary from low, creeping plants to stately clumps with tall, spike-like racemes of crowded flowers. The 5-petalled flowers are mostly yellow or white, less commonly pink or purple.

CULTIVATION Plant in slightly acidic soil with a good mix of organic matter and medium to moist conditions in sun or part-shade. Propagate from seed or cuttings, or by division.

Lysimachia vulgaris
Yellow loosestrife

A common wildflower in Europe and western Asia, it grows in wet meadows and along streams. It is a perennial, with creeping rhizomes and tall stems, 4 ft (1.2 m) or more in height, with broad green leaves in whorls of three or four. In summer, golden-yellow star-shaped flowers about ¾ in (18 mm) wide are borne in loose terminal spikes. Plant at the water's edge of a pond or stream.

ZONES 5–10.

Lysimachia vulgaris

MNO

MECONOPSIS

This genus is known for its large, exotic flowers with papery petals and a bold, central boss of stamens borne on tall stems. The flower stalks lengthen after flowering as the fruits develop. The hairy leaves are either simple or pinnate. In all, there are about 45 species of annuals, biennials and short-lived perennials.

CULTIVATION Plant in a cool, shady or semi-shaded site, and protect from strong winds. Mostly frost hardy, they need a moist but not over-wet, lime-free, humus-rich soil. Propagate from seed in late summer.

Meconopsis cambrica
Welsh poppy

Native to western Europe and the UK, this species has slightly hairy, deeply divided, mid-green leaves which form basal rosettes, and lemon yellow or rich orange flowers in mid-spring to fall (autumn).

Meconopsis grandis

Meconopsis cambrica

It has a spreading habit, reaching 12–18 in (30–45 cm) tall and 12 in (30 cm) wide. Though short lived, it self-seeds readily, given the right conditions.

ZONES 6–10.

Meconopsis grandis
Himalayan blue poppy

This magnificent rich blue poppy is more solidly perennial than other species of the genus. It has rosettes of irregularly toothed, deciduous green leaves with red-brown or rust colored hairs. The brilliant, early summer flowers can be up to 6 in (15 cm) across on stems up to 4 ft (1.2 m) tall.

ZONES 5–9.

MIMULUS

syn. *Diplacus*
Monkey flower, musk

The snapdragon-like flowers of this genus are tubular, with flared mouths, often curiously spotted and mottled; they come in a range of colors including brown, orange, yellow, red, pink and crimson. The common name refers to the alleged resemblance to a grinning monkey. The 180 or so species of annuals, perennials and shrubs of this genus are mainly native to the cool Pacific coastal areas of Chile and the USA. Most species are suited to bog gardens or other moist situations, although some make successful rock garden plants.

Mimulus moschatus

CULTIVATION Grow these plants in full sun or part-shade in wet or moist soil. Propagate perennials by division in spring and annuals from seed in fall (autumn) or early spring.

Mimulus moschatus
Monkey musk

Although once grown for its musk scent, this species has been mysteriously odourless for many years. It is a small, creeping, water-loving perennial which grows to a height and spread of 6-12 in (15–30 cm). Its pale yellow flowers, lightly dotted with brown, appear in summer to fall (autumn). It is very frost hardy.

ZONES 7–10.

MONARDA
Bergamot, horsemint

The leaves and flowers of Bergamot are used medicinally and to flavor teas and add scent to potpourris; the flowers are valued both for their beauty and their fragrance. This is a North American genus of 15 species of perennials and annuals with green, sometimes purple-tinged, veined, aromatic leaves and flowers borne in whorls from mid-summer to early fall (autumn). The plants may be sparsely branching, or single-stemmed.

CULTIVATION These plants are very frost hardy and best planted in full sun although they will tolerate some shade. Perennials prefer

Monarda didyma

Monarda didyma 'Aquarius'

moist, well-drained soil and in some climates respond to a good feed of manure or compost. Propagate perennials by division of established clumps, annuals by seed sown *in situ* in sandy, well-drained soil.

Monarda didyma
Bee balm, Oswego tea

Used by the Native Americans and early colonists as a herbal tea and the young leaves useful in salads or as a stuffing for roast meat, this is one of the showiest of the culinary herbs. In late summer, it produces spidery white, pink or red flowers, and it may grow at least 3 ft (1 m) tall. Cultivars include **'Aquarius'** (deep, purple-lilac flowers with purplish green bracts), **'Cambridge Scarlet'** (its dark green leaves emit an exotic, citrus-like scent when crushed) and **'Croftway Pink'** (rose-pink flowers).

ZONES 4–10.

Useful Tip

To attract bees into your garden, grow perennials such as foxgloves, Helenium, Kniphofia, Liatris spicata, Nepeta, Scabiosa *and aromatic herbs including bergamot, oregano, rosemary,* Stachys *(sage) and thyme.*

NEPETA

These plants are grown in herbaceous borders and as ground cover or edging; many species, of which there are over 200, have aromatic, silver-gray foliage and a compact growing habit, others are taller and may need to be supported. Many species have been extensively hybridized to produce exceptional garden plants. Largely perennial, rarely annual, these plants originate from a wide area of Eurasia, North Africa and the mountains of tropical Africa.

CULTIVATION They thrive in a well-drained soil in a sunny site. Some of the vigorous herbaceous species make good single species ground covers as they have a tendency to overpower less robust plants. Keep such plants in check by trimming lightly during the growing season and cutting back each year to prevent the plants from becoming straggly. Propagate by division, from cuttings taken during late spring, or from seed.

Nepeta x *faassenii*
Catmint

Catmint is particularly attractive against a backdrop of stone, whether it be a garden wall, paving, or rockery. The gray-green foliage, aromatic when crushed, contrasts with an abundance of small, violet-blue flowers throughout

Nepeta x *faassenii*

summer. A bushy, clump-forming perennial, useful for separating strong colours in the shrub or flower border, it achieves a height and spread of 18 in (45 cm). Many cultivars are available, including **'Dropmore Blue'**, **'Six Hills Giant'** and **'Walker's Blue'**, which has finer foliage and flowers than the other 2 hybrids.

ZONES 3–10.

NIEREMBERGIA

Cupflower

These slender plants with generally fine foliage and cup-shaped flowers are found growing naturally in moist, sunny places in the more temperate regions of South America. Comprising 23 species within the Solanaceae family, these annual and perennial herbs and subshrubs make ideal plants for borders or rock garden pockets where the somewhat invasive species (such as *Nierembergia repens*) can be contained. Flowers come in a variety of colors, the most popular garden species bearing white or purple-blue flowers.

CULTIVATION They do best in well-composted soil in full sun. To prolong the flowering period, water well and feed. In colder areas, treat the perennials as annuals, but in milder climates they can be overwintered outdoors. Propagate perennials by division in spring, annuals from seed and subshrubs from cuttings towards late summer.

Nierembergia repens
syn. *Nierembergia rivularis*
Whitecup

This perennial species is best grown in a defined area, such as paving crevices or a rock garden as it may become invasive, spreading by underground stems to form clumps of about 2 in (5 cm) high by 18 in (45 cm) wide. A mat-forming plant with small, spoon-shaped and bright green leaves, it does best in dry, sandy soil. A profusion of single, open flowers, white with a golden center, are a summer feature.

ZONES 8–10.

Nierembergia repens

OENOTHERA

Evening primrose

Evening primrose oil, which is extracted from the tiny seeds of *Oenothera biennis*, contains certain fatty acids believed to be beneficial to health if consumed regularly in modest quantities. This is a genus of more than 120 species of annuals, biennials and perennials originally from temperate regions of both North and South America but widely naturalized elsewhere. In summer, their delicate flowers—each with 4 petals and a long basal tube—open at dawn or dusk and fade rapidly. They may be yellow, red, white or (less commonly) pink. Most species are pollinated by nocturnal insects and only release their fragrance at night; the flowers of some do not even open during the day.

CULTIVATION Mostly frost hardy, they do best in a well-drained, sandy soil in an open, sunny position. They will tolerate dry conditions. Propagate from seed or by division in spring or fall (autumn), or from softwood cuttings in late spring.

Oenothera speciosa
White evening primrose, showy evening primrose

This native of southern USA and Mexico bears an abundance of fragrant, cup-shaped, pink-tinted white flowers, fresh flowerheads opening daily all summer long. The small leaves of this short-lived, clump-forming perennial often turn red in hot or cold weather. It grows to 18-24 in (45–60 cm) in height with a spread of 18 in (45 cm) or more. The cultivar **'Rosea'** (syns 'Childsii', *Oenothera berlandieri*) is lower growing, with yellow-centered flowers edged and heavily veined in rose pink. **'Siskiyou'** is similar but has larger flowers. These pink forms should not be confused with *O. rosea*, which has much smaller flowers.

ZONES 5–10.

Oenothera speciosa 'Rosea'

OPHIOPOGON

Mondo grass, snakebeard, lilyturf

This genus comprises 50 or so species of evergreen perennials from eastern Asia. These trouble-free plants will last almost indefinitely, and are grown for their attractive, long-lasting clumps of grass-like foliage which rises from underground rhizomes. In fact, they are not grasses but lilies, allied to *Convallaria* (lily-of-the-valley). In summer, leafless stems bear racemes of numerous small, semi-spherical to bell-shaped flowers in white or blue through to purple. The glossy, blue or black, berry-like fruits each contain one seed.

CULTIVATION Most are fairly frost hardy and will tolerate sun or part-shade in moist, well-drained soil. Propagate by division of clumps in spring, or from seed in fall (autumn). For a quick, attractive ground cover, plant divisions at intervals of 8 in (20 cm).

Ophiopogon planiscapus **'Nigrescens'**
syn. 'Ebony Night'
Black mondo grass

This Japanese cultivar is grown for its distinctive, purple-black, rather stiff leaves about ¼ in (6 mm) wide, which form slow-growing, sparse clumps. Its lilac flowers appear in clusters along the flowering stem in summer. These are followed by black fruit. It reaches a height of 10 in (25 cm) and a spread of 12 in (30 cm).

ZONES 6–10.

Ophiopogon planiscapus 'Nigrescens'

P

PAEONIA

Peony

Paeonia derives from classical Greek and refers to the medicinal properties attributed to some of the 33 species of beautiful perennials and shrubs in this genus. All are deciduous and have long-lived, rather woody rootstocks with swollen roots and large compound leaves with leaflets which are usually toothed or lobed. In spring, each new stem bears one to several large, rose-like flowers, their centers a mass of short stamens that almost conceal the ovaries. Flowers are mostly in shades of pink or red, although white- and yellow-flowered species exist. Most are herbaceous and die back to the ground in fall (autumn), but the small group of Chinese 'tree peonies' have woody stems up to about 8 ft (2.4 m) in height, so strictly they are shrubs. Tree peony cultivars produce the most flamboyant flowers, some as large as 12 in (30 cm) across, mostly double and often frilled or ruffled.

Paeonia lactiflora 'Cora Stubbs'

CULTIVATION Most need a cold winter, allowing dormancy and initiation of flower buds, but a late frost will damage new foliage and flower buds. They like a sheltered site in full or slightly filtered sun, and cool, moist soil. Mulch and feed with well-rotted manure when leaf growth starts, but avoid disturbing roots. Pruning of the tree peonies should be minimal, consisting of trimming out weaker side shoots. Propagate from seed in fall (autumn), or by division in the case of named cultivars.

Paeonia lactiflora Hybrids

These herbaceous Chinese hybrids have maroon-tinted foliage when it first appears in spring, and often fragrant flowers in a wide range of colors and forms: **'Beacon Flame'** (deep red, semi-double); **'Bowl of Beauty'** (creamy white and pale pink); **'Coral Charm'** (deep apricot buds fading to soft orange-pink); **'Cora Stubbs'** (contrasting tones); **'Duchesse de Nemours'** (scented white to soft yellow); **'Félix Crousse'** (deep pink double, red center); **'Festiva Maxima'** (fully double, scented, frilled white, red flecks); **'Inspecteur Lavergne'** (fully double red); **'Kelway's Glorious'** (scented, creamy white, double); **'Miss America'** (scented white, gold stamens); **'Monsieur Jules Elie'** (deep cerise-pink, single); **'President Roosevelt'** ('rose' or 'bomb' double); **'Sarah Bernhardt'** (scented rose pink, silver-margined, double); and **'Whitleyi Major'** (single, ivory-white, yellow stamens).

ZONES 6–9.

Useful Tip

While many perennials should be divided every 2-3 years, peonies are happier left undisturbed for longer and, when you do divide them, will take a while to recover.

Paeonia lactiflora hybrid 'Beacon Flame'

PAPAVER

Poppy

Characteristic to the genus are nodding buds which open into wide, cup-shaped flowers facing the sky, followed by distinctive pepper-pot seed pods. The 50 or so annual, biennial or perennial species of the genus are mainly from the temperate parts of Eurasia and Africa, with a couple from eastern USA. The tree poppy (*Romneya*), the Californian poppy (*Eschscholzia*) and the blue poppy (*Meconopsis*) are related and share the common name.

CULTIVATION Poppies grow well in deep, moist, well-drained soil. They are fully frost hardy and prefer little or no shade. Sow seed in spring or fall (autumn); many species self-seed readily.

Papaver orientale
Oriental poppy

A native of southwest Asia, this herbaceous perennial bears spectacular summer flowers, as big as 4 in (10 cm) in diameter, in shades of pink through to red with dark centers. Cultivated varieties have a range of colors, many with a dark blotch on petal bases; some are even double. Leaves are hairy, lance-like and bluish green, and the plants can become straggly. Poppy varieties range from 18 in (45 cm) to more than 3 ft (1 m) tall. Cultivars include: '**China Boy**', '**Rosenwelle**', '**Feuerriese**', '**Cedric Morris**' and '**Mrs Perry**'.

ZONES 3–9.

Papaver orientale

PELARGONIUM

Geranium

Despite their common name, the popular hybrid pelargoniums in fact belong to the genus *Pelargonium*, which, though from the same family, is quite distinct from the *Geranium* genus. The genus *Pelargonium* consists of perhaps 280 species, the vast majority endemic to South Africa and adjacent Namibia. Most are soft-wooded shrubs and sub-shrubs, but the genus includes some herbaceous perennials and annuals; a number of species even have succulent stems, leaves or roots and are grown by succulent collectors. The leaves may be toothed, scalloped, lobed or dis-sected, and are usually aromatic, containing a wide range of essential oils. They may secrete resin droplets that give the leaves a sticky feel. The upper 2 petals of wild *Pelargonium* flowers are colored or marked differently from the 3 lower ones, a feature that distinguishes pelargoniums from true geraniums. Their seeds are plumed like thistledown, another distinguishing feature.

The commonly-grown hybrid groups are: **Zonal pelargoniums, Ivy-leaved pelargoniums, Regal pelargoniums, Unique pelargoniums, Angel pelargoniums** and finally **Scented-leaved pelargoniums**, grown for their fragrant foliage, some being grown commercially for 'geranium oil'.

Pelargonium, Regal Hybrid, 'Rosmaroy'

CULTIVATION In warmer climates with long daylight hours, they flower almost all the time, but they are intolerant of extreme heat and humidity. In colder climates, they are often treated as annuals, being frost-tender. Plant in a sunny site with light, well-drained, neutral soil; avoid overwatering. If grown in pots, deadhead and fertilize regularly. Propagate from softwood cuttings from spring to fall (autumn).

Pelargonium, Regal Hybrids
Martha Washington geraniums, regal geraniums, regal pelargoniums

The spectacular flowers of these hybrids make them popular for flower shows and as potted plants. Originally derived from a mauve-flowering species, breeding with other species has resulted in red, purple and white colors too. Forming a shrub about 24 in (60 cm) high, they have strong woody stems and stiff, pleated, sharply-toothed leaves. Large, wide open, often blotched or bicolored flowers appear in late spring and summer. In cool climates, protect plants from frost. Trim back hard after blooming to keep the bush compact. Cultivars include: **'Grand Slam'**, **'Kimono'**, **'Lord Bute'**, **'Lyewood Bonanza'**, **'Monkwood Bonanza'**, **'Morwenna'** (syn. 'Morweena'), **'Parisienne'**, **'Rembrandt'**, **'Rosmaroy'**, **'Spot-on-Bonanza'**, **'Vicky Clare'**, **'White Glory'** and **'Starlight'**.

ZONES 9–11.

Pelargonium, Regal Hybrid, 'Lyewood Bonanza'

PENSTEMON

This genus consists of 250 species of deciduous, evergreen or semi-evergreen subshrubs and perennials, most of them native to Central and North America. Hybrids are grown for their spikes of foxglove-like flowers in blues, reds, whites and bicolors. The leaves appear in opposite pairs or whorls, while the flowers have 2 lobes on the upper lip and 3 on the lower. Grow tall varieties in sheltered borders and dwarf strains in rock gardens or as bedding. **'Bev Jensen'** is red and **'Holly's White'** is a favorite in the USA.

CULTIVATION Marginally to very frost-hardy, these plants thrive in fertile, well-drained soil and full sun. Cut plants back hard after flowering. They can be propagated from seed in spring or fall (autumn), by division in spring, or from cuttings of non-flowering shoots in late summer (the only method for cultivars).

Penstemon heterophyllus
Foothill penstemon, blue bedder penstemon

A summer-flowering subshrub reaching about 18 in (45 cm) in height, this very frost-hardy species grows wild in California. Its leaves are 1–2 in (2.5–5 cm) long, lance-shaped and slightly blue-green. The flowers vary from deep violet-pink to near blue and may be 1–1½ in (25–35 mm) long. The semi-evergreen shrub *Penstemon heterophyllus* subsp. *purdyi* (syn. *P. h.* 'Blue Bedder') has blue, tubular flowers and pale green leaves.

ZONES 8–10.

Penstemon heterophyllus

PERICALLIS

Cineraria

Well-known for the florists' cineraria (*Pericallis* x *hybrida*), which is available in a multitude of colors, the wild plants of the genus —which comprises about 15 species of perennials and subshrubs closely allied to *Senecio*, where they were once included—are not nearly as extravagant. They grow throughout the mid-latitude islands of the Atlantic Ocean. The leaves, which form basal rosettes in the perennials, are covered in fine hairs, and are often oval to lance-shaped, 2-6 in (5–15 cm) long, with finely-toothed edges. The daisy-like flowers are usually pink, mauve or purple, about ½-2 in (1.2–5 cm) wide and carried singly or in corymbs.

CULTIVATION Easy to grow in any moist, well-drained soil in part- to full shade. Almost all are frost tender. The florists' strains are often used as winter-flowering house plants. Propagate from seed or cuttings or by division, depending on the growth form.

Pericallis x *hybrida*
syns *Senecio cruentus*,
S. x *hybrida*

A multi-purpose plant, ideal for window boxes, containers on balconies or in courtyards, as well as

Pericallis x *hybrida*

for formal bedding in part-shaded spots, this hybrid reaches 12 in (30 cm) tall and wide. The flowers range from the traditional blue through pink, red, purple and crimson to white. Although very tolerant of heat, salt air and poor soil, they do not like high humidity or excessive rain.
ZONES 9–11.

PHLOX

These are some of the brightest of the summer flowers; the botanical name, meaning 'flame', is highly appropriate. The genus comprises more than 60 species of evergreen and semi-evergreen annuals and perennials, most of them native to North America. The abundant

Phlox paniculata 'Mother of Pearl'

flowers are both fragrant and showy, making phlox popular for borders and bedding displays.

CULTIVATION The perennials are easily grown in any temperate climate and need a lot of water while they grow. Annuals grow in almost any climate. Plant in full sun or semi-shade, in fertile, moist but well-drained soil. Propagate from seed or cuttings or by division. Red spider mite, eelworm and powdery mildew can be a problem.

Phlox paniculata
Summer phlox, perennial phlox

This summer-flowering perennial grows to 3 ft (1 m), and bears long-lasting flowerheads of many small flowers in a range of colors, depending on the cultivar: blue through to violet ('**Amethyst**', '**Eventide**'); shades of pink ('**Mother of Pearl**', '**Windsor**', '**Sir John Falstaff**'); white ('**Fujiyama**', '**Snow Hare**', '**White Admiral**'); and bicolors ('**Brigadier**', '**Bright Eyes**', '**Graf Zeppelin**', '**Prince of Orange**', '**Prospero**').

ZONES 4–10.

PHORMIUM
New Zealand flax

The fiber of these flax plants from New Zealand has in time past been used commercially, but is now mainly confined to Maori crafts. The genus has only 2 species, valued for the dramatic effect of their large, arching, striped leaves which may be anything from dark green to green-yellow; variegated or brightly colored cultivars exist. They form large clumps and grow well in most conditions. In summer, the panicles of flowers attract nectar-feeding birds. They range in height from 3 ft (1 m) to 6 ft (1.8 m).

CULTIVATION These versatile plants make striking container plants as well as useful garden specimens in almost any climate. They are fairly frost hardy and respond well to generous watering

Phormium Hybrid 'Rainbow Warrior'

and permanently moist conditions. Propagate from seed or by division in spring.

Phormium Hybrids

'Rainbow Warrior' is a recently released cultivar that makes a luxuriant clump of foliage. Its long, arching and drooping leaves are mainly pinkish red and are irregularly striped with bronze green.

ZONES 8–11.

Useful Tip

Nectar–feeding birds will feast on the kangaroo paw, Kniphofia *and* Phormium *growing in your garden.*

PHYSOSTEGIA

Obedient plant, false dragon head

The common name refers to the fact that if a flower is moved, it will stay put and won't spring back. A North American genus of some 12 species of rhizomatous perennials, these plants are vigorous and rapidly form clumps of unbranched, upright stems clothed in narrow, lance-shaped leaves with toothed edges. Height varies from 2-6 ft (0.6–1.8 m) and the leaves are 2-6 in (5–15 cm) long. Tubular to bell-shaped flowers in shades of lavender, pink or purple and white appear on spikes from mid-summer. They are usually less than ½ in (12 mm) long.

CULTIVATION Very easy to grow, they prefer moist, well-drained soil in sun or very light shade. They can be slightly invasive. Frost hardiness varies, though all are tolerant of moderate frosts. Propagate from seed, from small basal cuttings or by division.

Physostegia virginiana

This herbaceous perennial, a native of eastern and central North America, grows to 3 ft (1m) and produces a stunning display of flower spikes in late summer. The flowers may be white ('**Summer Snow**'), magenta ('**Vivid**') or pink ('**Summer Spire**').

ZONES 3–10.

Physostegia virginiana 'Summer Spire'

PLATYCODON

Balloon flower, Chinese bellflower

There is only one species in this genus—a semi-tuberous perennial with flower stems up to 30 in (75 cm) tall. It is native to China, Japan, Korea and eastern Siberia. In spring, it forms a neat clump of long, toothed-edged, elliptical to lance-shaped light blue-green leaves, each leaf about 2-3 in (5-8 cm) long. The leafy flower stems develop quickly from mid-summer, and are topped with balloon-like buds that open into broad, bell-shaped, white, pink, blue or purple flowers up to 5 cm (2 in) wide.

CULTIVATION Very frost hardy and easily grown in any well-drained soil in full sun, this plant may nonetheless take a few years to become established. Propagate from seed or by division. It resents disturbance, so divide it as little as possible.

Platycodon grandiflorus 'Fuji Blue'

Platycodon grandiflorus

The balloon-like buds appear in summer. The serrated, elliptical leaves have a silvery blue cast and form a neat clump up to 24 in (60 cm) in height and 12 in (30 cm) in spread. *Platycodon grandiflorus* var. *Mariesii* reaches only 18 in (45 cm) in height and has glossy, lance-shaped leaves. **'Fuji Blue'** is very erect, as much as 30 in (75 cm) tall, and bears large blue flowers.

ZONES 4–10.

POTENTILLA

Cinquefoil

Some species in this genus are used medicinally: the root bark of one species, for example, is said to stop nosebleeds and even internal bleeding. The 5-part leaves of most of the species give this large genus its common name. About 500 perennials, annuals, biennials and deciduous shrubs make up the genus, and are distributed from temperate to arctic regions, mainly in the northern hemisphere.

Plants vary from only 1 in (25 mm) to about 18 in (45 cm) tall. A profusion of rounded, bright flowers are borne in clusters from spring through to summer.

CULTIVATION Plants thrive in well-drained, fertile soil and in full sun in temperate climates, although it is worth remembering that pink, red and orange cultivars will be brighter if protected from very strong sun. They are tolerant of lime and the perennials are generally frost hardy. Propagate by division in spring, or from seed or by division in fall (autumn). Shrubs can be propagated from seed in fall (autumn) or from cuttings in summer.

Potentilla nepalensis

A native of the Himalayas, this perennial is grown for its profusion of flowers in shades of pink or apricot with cherry red centers. Flowering takes place all summer long. Plants have bright green, strawberry-like leaves, grow to 12 in (30 cm) or more in height and spread about 24 in (60 cm). **'Miss**

Potentilla nepalensis

Willmott' is a cultivar with deep pink flowers which grows about 18 in (45 cm) high.

ZONES 5–9.

PRIMULA

Primrose

About 400 species belong in this genus which is distributed throughout the temperate regions of the northern hemisphere, mainly concentrated in China and the Himalayas. They also grow wild on high mountains in the tropics, as far south as Papua New Guinea. Although mainly rhizomatous, some have poorly developed rhizomes and are short lived. There is often a basal tuft or rosette of leaves, which have toothed or scalloped margins and are usually broadest toward their tips. The flowering stems vary, mostly carrying successive whorls or a single umbel of flowers; a few species bear flowers tightly crowded into a terminal head or a short spike, others, singly or in small groups on short stalks from among the leaves. Flower shape, size and color vary widely; generally, flowers are tubular, opening into a funnel or flat disc with at least 5 petals, often notched at the tips.

CULTIVATION They thrive in fertile, well-drained soil and they like part-shade and ample water. Deadhead and trim back foliage after flowering. Sow seed in spring, early summer or fall (autumn), or propagate by division or from root cuttings.

Primula, Polyanthus Group

Primula,
Polyanthus Group
syn. *Primula* x *polyantha*

Cultivated since the seventeenth century, these cultivars are derived from *Primula vulgaris* crossed with *P. veris*. They are fully frost-hardy perennials, sometimes grown as annuals, and reach 12 in (30 cm) in spread and height. From winter to spring they bear large, flat, scented flowers on dense umbels in every color except green.

ZONES 6–10.

PULMONARIA
Lungwort

The rather ugly common name of this genus derives from their former medicinal use, not their appearance. A Eurasian genus consisting of 14 species of perennial, rhizomatous, forget-me-not-like plants which grow in a variety of habitats, from mountains, to woodland and beside streams, the most common species are low, spreading plants 6-10 in (15–25 cm) high with a spread of at least 24 in (60 cm). The simple, oval to lanceolate leaves are sometimes slightly downy and often spotted silver-white. From very early spring, small deep blue, pink or white flowers open from pink or white buds.

CULTIVATION These plants are easily grown in cool, moist, humus-rich soil in light shade. They are all very frost hardy. Trim off old leaves after blooming. Propagate from seed or cuttings or by division after flowering or in fall (autumn).

Pulmonaria saccharata
Jerusalem sage,
Bethlehem sage

An evergreen clump-forming perennial with heavily spotted, hairy leaves about 10 in (25 cm) in length, this species has given rise to numerous cultivars with flowers in white and many shades of pink and blue. 'Highdown' is 12 in (30 cm) tall and has silver-frosted leaves and pendulous clusters of blue flowers. The cultivars of the **Argentea Group** have silver leaves and red flowers that age to dark purple.

ZONES 3–9.

Pulmonaria saccharata 'Highdown'

PULSATILLA

Pasque flower

The plants in this genus are grown for their ferny foliage and their solitary, often downy, cup-like flowers. The 30 species of spring-flowering, deciduous perennials are native to Eurasia and North America. The plants are mound forming, and the leaves and flower stems are covered with downy silver-gray hairs; the general effect being that of a hairy anemone with large flowers. The flower colors range from white through pink and purple to red.

CULTIVATION Very frost hardy, these plants do best with cool to cold winters and cool summers and tend to be short lived in mild areas. They prefer a moist, gritty, scree soil in sun or part-shade, but resent being too wet in winter. Although mostly grown in rockeries, they are also useful in borders and troughs. Propagate from seed or by division.

Pulsatilla alpina subsp. *apiifolia*

This palest yellow-flowered form of a normally white-flowered species is found through much of southern Europe and the Caucasus. It usually favors slightly acid soil. Flower stems may be 18 in (45 cm) tall and flowers as wide as 2 in (5cm).

ZONES 5–9.

Useful Tip

Pulsatillas do not like to have their roots disturbed, so plant them when they are fairly small and then leave them alone.

Pulsatilla alpina subsp. *apiifolia*

RST

REHMANNIA

The exact grouping of these Chinese perennials is somewhat vague: they are sometimes classed with the foxgloves and the snapdragons, at other times, grouped as cousins of the African violet. This is because their 2-lipped flowers look a little like foxgloves, snapdragons and African violets. *Rehmannia* flowers are borne in terminal racemes and are very attractive, usually some shade of cool pink, with pink and gold at their throats. The leaves form basal rosettes and are large, oblong, conspicuously veined and hairy.

CULTIVATION In a warm-temperate climate, choose a sheltered site in full sun (or a gently-warmed greenhouse in cool climates) and provide a rich, leafy soil. Propagate from seed in winter or cuttings in late fall (autumn). Watch for attack by slugs and snails.

Rehmannia elata
syn. *Rehmannia angulata*
of gardens
Chinese foxglove

This is the best known *Rehmannia* and, though perennial, is only short lived. It bears semi-pendent, tubular, bright pink flowers from summer to fall (autumn) and grows up to 3 ft (1 m) high.

ZONES 9–10.

Rehmannia elata

Useful Tip

Introduce fish to your pond and let them take care of the mosquito larvae.

RUDBECKIA

Coneflower, marmalade daisy

The plants in this popular genus have bright, daisy-like, composite flowers with prominent central cones, similar to *Echinacea* (hence the shared common name). The genus includes about 15 species of annuals, biennials and perennials native to the moist meadows and light woodlands of North America. The single, double or semi-double flowers are usually in tones of yellow; the cones vary from green through rust, purple and black. Species vary in height from 24 in (60 cm) to up to 10 ft (3 m). A number of rudbeckias make excellent cut flowers.

CULTIVATION   Coneflowers like full sun or part-shade and prefer loamy, moisture-retentive soil. They are moderately to fully frost hardy. Propagate from seed or by division in spring or fall (autumn). Aphids may be a problem.

Rudbeckia laciniata
Cutleaf coneflower

This delightful summer-flowering perennial can reach 10 ft (3 m) in height, though plants of 6 ft (1.8 m) are more common. The drooping ray florets give the flowerhead an informal elegance. **'Golden Glow'** is a striking, if somewhat floppy, double cultivar. **'Goldquelle'** grows to around 30 in (75 cm) tall and has large, bright yellow, double flowers.

ZONES 3–10.

Rudbeckia laciniata

Rudbeckia laciniata 'Goldquelle'

SALVIA

Sage

The name Salvia dates back to Roman times and derives from the Latin *salvus*, meaning 'safe' or 'well'. This is likely to be a reference to the healing properties attributed to *Salvia officinalis*, the common sage: it is said to be a tonic, and good for sore throats. The aromatic leaves of some species are grown as culinary herbs, used in stuffing and as part of the *bouquet garni*, but even these plants are pleasantly ornamental. This, the largest genus of the mint family, consists of about 900 species of annuals, perennials and soft-wooded shrubs, represented in most parts of the world except very cold regions and tropical rainforests. The tubular, 2-lipped flowers are very distinctive, the lower lip being flat and the upper lip forming a helmet or boat shape; the 2-lipped calyx may also be colored. The flower colors include some of the brightest blues and scarlets of any plants, though yellow is rare.

CULTIVATION Although some of the perennials are reasonably frost-hardy, most of the shrubby Mexican and South American species will tolerate only light frosts. Sages tend to do best planted in full sun in well drained, light-textured soil with adequate watering in summer. Propagate from seed in spring, cuttings in early summer, or division of rhizomatous species at almost any time. Snails, slugs and caterpillars attack many species.

Salvia x sylvestris

This leafy perennial, which grows to 12–36 in (30–90 cm) tall, is a cross between *Salvia pratensis* and *S. nemorosa*. It comes from western Asia and Europe but is naturalized in North America. Its oblong, heart-shaped leaves are 2–4 in (5–10 cm) long and hairy. In summer, purplish-violet flowers appear in long-branched heads. The many cultivars include: *'Blauhügel'* ('Blue Mound'), **'Ostfriesland'** ('East Friesland'), **'Mainacht'** and **'Wesuwe'**.

ZONES 5–10.

Salvia x *sylvestris* 'Ostfriesland'

SCABIOSA

Scabious, pincushion flower

The tall-stemmed, honey-scented blooms of this genus have multiple florets and protruding filaments giving a pincushion effect, and range in color from white, yellow, red, blue and mauve to deep purple. This is a genus of 80 annuals, biennials and perennials from sunny sites, dry slopes and meadows in temperate climates (mainly in the Mediterranean, but also the rest of Europe, Africa, Asia and Japan). Taller perennials are ideal for the wildflower garden, while shorter species suit rock gardens; annuals are excellent in borders.

CULTIVATION Grow in full sun in well-drained, alkaline soil. Propagate annuals from seed in spring and perennials from cut-tings in summer, seed in fall (autumn) or by division in early spring.

Scabiosa caucasica

The summer flowers of this perennial come in many colors and often have a contrasting center. It reaches a height and spread of 18-24 in (45–60 cm). Cultivars include: '**Clive Greaves**' (lilac-blue); '**Miss Wilmott**' (white); '**Staefa**' (vigorous, blue); and '**Mrs Isaac House**' (creamy white).

ZONES 4–10.

Top: *Scabiosa caucasica*
Above: *Scabiosa caucasica* 'Staefa'

Scabiosa caucasica 'Mrs Isaac House'

STACHYS

Betony, woundwort, hedge nettle

The members of this genus, which belongs to the mint family, have long been used in herb gardens and many of them are believed to have medicinal value; today, betony is mainly used in herbal teas. This genus contains about 300 species of annuals, perennials and evergreen shrubs from a range of habitats mostly in northern temperate regions. Many species are aromatic and most are attractive to bees and butterflies. They bear tubular, 2-lipped, purple, red, pink, yellow or white flowers.

CULTIVATION They prefer well-drained, moderately fertile soil in full sun. Propagate from seed or cuttings or by division.

Stachys byzantina

syns *Stachys lanata, S. olympica*
Lambs' ears, lambs' tails, lambs' tongues

The lance-shaped, white, downy leaves of this perennial species are reminiscent of lambs' tongues, hence its common name. Unfortunately, the leaves turn to mush in very cold, humid or wet weather. A successful ground cover or border plant, this species grows to 12–18 in (30–45 cm) high, with a 24 in (60 cm) spread. Mauve-pink flowers appear in summer. The cultivars are quite distinct: **'Silver Carpet'** (seldom flowers, remaining more compact than the species); **'Cotton Boll'** syn. 'Sheila McQueen' (flowers like cotton bolls); **'Primrose Heron'** (yellowish green leaves); and **'Big Ears'** syn. 'Countess Helen von Stein' (large-growing, with tall spikes of purple flowers).

ZONES 5–10.

Stachys byzantina

Useful Tip

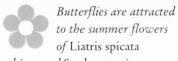

Butterflies are attracted to the summer flowers of Liatris spicata *scabious and* Stachys *species.*

STOKESIA

Stokes' aster

This genus of a single perennial species originally from southeastern regions of the USA was named after Briton Dr Jonathan Stokes (1755–1831). It makes a very good cutting flower, as it bears flowers on long, erect stems. A late-flowering but rewarding perennial, it can grow to about 18 in (45 cm) high and flowers from late summer to fall (autumn) if the spent flower stems are promptly removed.

CULTIVATION This plant likes full sun or part-shade and light, fertile, well-drained soil; it may rot in damp, heavy soil. It needs plenty of water in summer and tall plants may need support. Propagate from seed in fall (autumn) or by division in spring.

Stokesia laevis

Stokesia laevis
syn. *Stokesia cyanea*

The blue-mauve or white blooms have a shaggy appearance reminiscent of cornflowers and are borne freely on erect stems. This fully frost-hardy perennial has evergreen rosettes of narrow, mid-green, basal and divided leaves. **'Blue Star'** and **'Silver Moon'** are two cultivars with light blue and silvery-white flowerheads, respectively.

ZONES 7–10.

TANACETUM
syn. *Pyrethrum*

In classical Greek mythology Ganymede drank a potion of tansy, a species of this genus, and became immortal. Despite being potentially quite poisonous even when applied externally, it has been used in recent times for promoting menstruation and treating skin conditions, sprains, bruises, 'hysteria' and rheumatism. The some 70 species, relatives of the chrysanthemum, are mainly confined to temperate regions of the northern hemisphere. They are grown for their daisy-like flowers and their foliage, which is often white-hairy and in many cases finely dissected. Many of the perennials have strongly aromatic foliage, which can be used in pot pourri.

CULTIVATION Moderately to very frost hardy, they like a position in full sun and well-drained, dryish soil; in fact, they do not do well in soil that is wet and heavy, so do not overwater. Deadhead to encourage a second flush of flowers. These plants spread readily and need to be kept under control. Propagate by division in spring or from seed in late winter or early spring.

Tanacetum niveum
Silver tansy

This appealing species has deeply divided gray-green leaves and grows to about 24 in (60 cm) with a spread of up to 3 ft (1 m). In mid-summer it produces a mass of small white flowerheads with yellow centers. This striking ornamental will successfully self-seed when grown in a border.
ZONES 7–10.

THALICTRUM
Meadow rue

The plants in this genus are grown for their attractive foliage and fluffy, showy flowers. Over 300 species of perennials make up the genus. The branches of their slender, upstanding stems often intertwine and the leaves are finely divided. Flowering takes place in spring and summer. The flowers lack petals; instead they have 4 or 5 sepals and conspicuous stamen tufts. Thalictrums are good candidates for borders, especially as a foil for perennials with bolder blooms and foliage and they do well in the margins of bush gardens.

CULTIVATION Frost hardy, these plants like to grow in sun or part-shade in any well-drained soil. Some species need cool conditions. Propagate from fresh seed in fall (autumn) or by division in spring.

Tanacetum niveum

Thalictrum delavayi

Thalictrum delavayi

syn. *Thalictrum dipterocarpum* of gardens
Lavender shower

This clump-forming perennial produces loose panicles of nodding, lilac flowers with prominent yellow stamens from the middle to the end of summer. The finely-divided leaves give the mid-green foliage a dainty appearance. Plants achieve a height of 4 ft (1.2 m) and a spread of 24 in (60 cm). The cultivar **'Hewitt's Double'** has mauve flowers with a rounded, pompon-like form.

ZONES 7–10.

TRADESCANTIA

syns *Rhoeo,
Setcreasea, Zebrina*
Spiderwort

This genus consists of 50 or more species of perennials, some of them evergreen, from North and South America. Some species are rather weedy, but the creeping species (wandering Jew) make useful ground covers and have attractive foliage. Some of the upright species are valued for their pure blue flowers, an elusive color in the late-summer garden. Most of the trailing types are rather frost tender and are usually grown as greenhouse pot plants. In mild-winter climates they make good ground cover, admired for their richly toned foliage.

CULTIVATION Grow in full sun or part-shade in fertile, moist to dry soil. They tend to become straggly, so it is important to cut them back ruthlessly. Propagate by division or from tip cuttings in spring, summer or fall (autumn).

Tradescantia pallida

syn. *Setcreasea purpurea*

This species from eastern Mexico forms a dense clump of foliage and has small pink flowers in summer. The leaves are slightly succulent and lance-shaped, about 3-6 in (8–15 cm) long, and they often develop red tints if grown in full sun. **'Purple Heart'** (syn. 'Purpurea') has purple foliage.

ZONES 8–11.

Tradescantia pallida 'Purple Heart'

V-Z

VERBASCUM

Mullein

Some 250 species make up this genus which is native to Europe and the temperate regions of Asia, mainly found on dry, stony hillsides, wasteland and open woodland; many species are no more than weeds. They include semi-evergreen to evergreen perennials, biennials as well as shrubs, including some very large and some very coarse species. Leaves range from glossy to velvety, hairy or even woolly and develop large, often complex, basal rosettes. Several species are valued for their stately habit, gray foliage and long summer-flowering season. The flowers open a few at a time along the spike.

CULTIVATION Although fully to moderately frost hardy, they are intolerant of cold and wet conditions. Choose an open, sunny location (although they do tolerate shade) with well-drained soil. Propagate from seed in spring or late summer or by division in winter. Some species self-seed readily.

Verbascum chaixii
Nettle-leaved mullein

This semi-evergreen perennial from southern Europe lives long enough to form clumps. The flowers, usually yellow, are borne on 3 ft (1 m) stems in summer and the leaves are rich green. **'Album'** is a finer, white-flowering cultivar. **ZONES 5–10.**

Verbascum chaixii

VERONICA

Speedwell

Medieval savants believed they could see a face in this flower, named after Saint Veronica, who is supposed to have wiped the face of Christ with her veil and been rewarded by having an image of His face left there. The shrubby species now have a genus of their own, *Hebe*, and all the remaining 200 or so are herbaceous perennials, ranging from prostrate, creeping plants ideal for the rock garden to giants of 6 ft (1.8 m). Small as the flowers are—no more than about ½ in (12 mm) wide—they make quite a display, being gathered in clusters of various sizes and blooming in great profusion during summer. Flowers are usually blue, although white and pink are also common.

CULTIVATION Fully to moderately frost hardy, these plants are easy to grow in any temperate climate and are not fussy about soil or position. Propagate from seed in fall (autumn) or spring, from cuttings in summer or by division in early spring or early fall (autumn).

Veronica austriaca
syn. *Veronica teucrium*

This clump-forming perennial grows to 10–18 in (25–45 cm) tall with long, slender stems bearing bright blue, saucer-shaped flowers in late spring. It is native to the grassland and open woods from southern Europe to northern Asia. Leaves vary from broadly oval to narrow and are either entire or deeply cut. Propagate by division in fall (autumn) or from softwood cuttings in summer. **'Crater Lake Blue'** is 12 in (30 cm) tall and has deep blue flowers; **'Royal Blue'** is taller with royal blue flowers. In late summer, *Veronica austriaca* subsp. *teucrium* bears flower stems 12 in (30 cm) high, with many tiny deep blue flowers; it prefers full sun and well-drained soil.

ZONES 6–10.

Veronica austriaca

VIOLA

Violet, heartsease, pansy

This genus of about 500 species of annuals, perennials and subshrubs is distributed throughout most temperate regions of the world, although the majority are found in North America, the Andes and Japan. They tend to be creeping plants, either deciduous or evergreen, with slender to thick rhizomes and often kidney- or heart-shaped leaves; in some species they have narrow lobes. The wild species have blooms no more than 1 in (25 mm) across and characteristically have 3 spreading lower petals and 2 erect upper petals, with a short nectar spur projecting to the rear of the flower. Many produce *cleistogamous* flowers, which have smaller petals that do not open properly and are able to set seed without cross-pollination. A few Eurasian species have been hybridized to produce garden pansies, violas and violettas with showy flowers in bright or deep colors. These are almost invariably grown as annuals, although some may be treated as short-lived perennials.

Useful Tip

 Stake tall plants, such as delphiniums and dahlias, to stop them toppling over.

Viola, Perennial Cultivar, 'Magic'

Viola, Perennial Cultivar, 'Jackanapes'

CULTIVATION They vary from moderately to fully frost hardy. The compact perennial species suit rock gardens, preferring cooler, moister sites, while the wider-spreading species make good ground covers beneath trees and taller shrubs and need very little attention. Pansies and violas (*Viola* x *wittrockiana*) are grown as annuals or pot plants in full sun and need shelter from drying winds. Propagate perennial species by division or from cuttings; annuals by seed sown in late winter or early spring, under glass if necessary, planting out in late spring in soil that is well drained but not too rich. Water well and feed sparingly as flowers develop.

Viola, Perennial Cultivars

These long-flowering, hardy perennials may bloom all year round in milder climates. They are derived primarily from *Viola lutea*, *V. amoena* and *V. cornuta*. 'Huntercombe Purple' has creamy centered purple flowers; 'Jackanapes' has brown upper petals and yellow lower petals; 'Maggie Mott' has bright purple-blue flowers; 'Nellie Britten' (syn. 'Haslemere') has lavender-pink flowers; and the purple 'Magic' flowers have a small eye of dark purple and yellow.

ZONES 6–10.

ZAUSCHNERIA

Four species of shrubby perennials make up this genus from southwestern USA and Mexico which is sometimes included in the *Epilobium* genus. They are grown for their masses of orange to scarlet, tubular flowers. Although very similar, for horticultural purposes they can be considered variations on *Zauschneria californica*.

CULTIVATION Marginally frost hardy, these species prefer a warm, sheltered position in full sun, and a well-drained soil. Propagate from seed or by division in spring, or from side-shoot cuttings in summer.

Zauschneria californica
syn. *Epilobium canum*
subsp. *canum*
Californian fuchsia

The common name is a reference both to the origin and the form of the flowers, which resemble those of the related fuschia. The bright red flowers are borne on terminal spikes on erect, slender stems in late summer and early fall (autumn). This evergreen shrub has lance-like leaves, 1 in (25 mm) long, is highly variable and grows 12–24 in (30–60 cm) tall and 3–6 ft (1–1.8 m) wide. It is undemanding, needing only occasional water and is hardy to around 15°F (–9°C). *Zauschneria californica* subsp. *cana* (syn. *Zauschneria cana*) is a small suckering shrub, growing 24 in (60 cm) high, with felty gray leaves and larger, vermilion flowers. *Z. c.* subsp. *canum* 'Dublin' (syn. 'Glasnevin') is a more compact plant only 12 in (30 cm) tall, with bright orange-red flowers.

ZONES 8–10.

Zauschneria californica

Useful Tip

The best time to pick flowers for vase arrangements is in the cool of the early morning, preferably before the sun has reached the garden.

HARDINESS ZONE MAPS

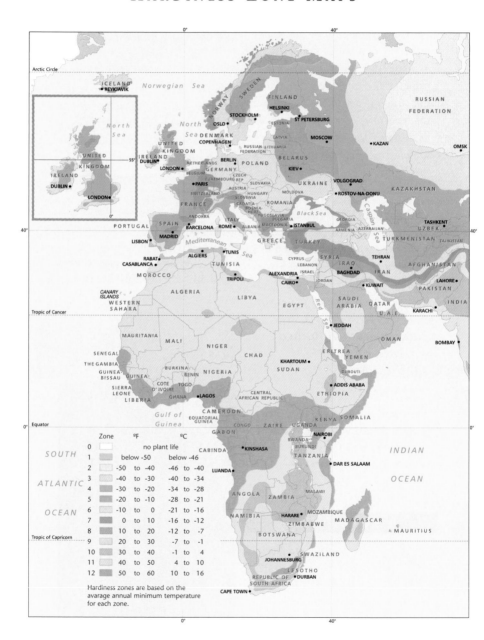

Zone	°F	°C
0	no plant life	
1	below -50	below -46
2	-50 to -40	-46 to -40
3	-40 to -30	-40 to -34
4	-30 to -20	-34 to -28
5	-20 to -10	-28 to -21
6	-10 to 0	-21 to -16
7	0 to 10	-16 to -12
8	10 to 20	-12 to -7
9	20 to 30	-7 to -1
10	30 to 40	-1 to 4
11	40 to 50	4 to 10
12	50 to 60	10 to 16

Hardiness zones are based on the avarage annual minimum temperature for each zone.

Note: The scale of this map differs from that of the following two maps.

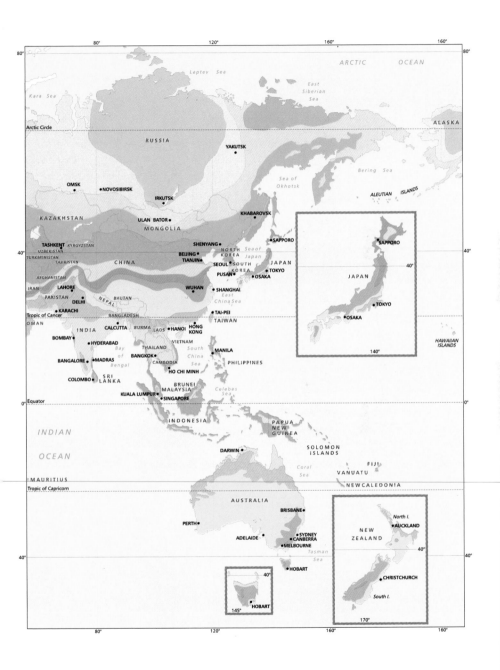

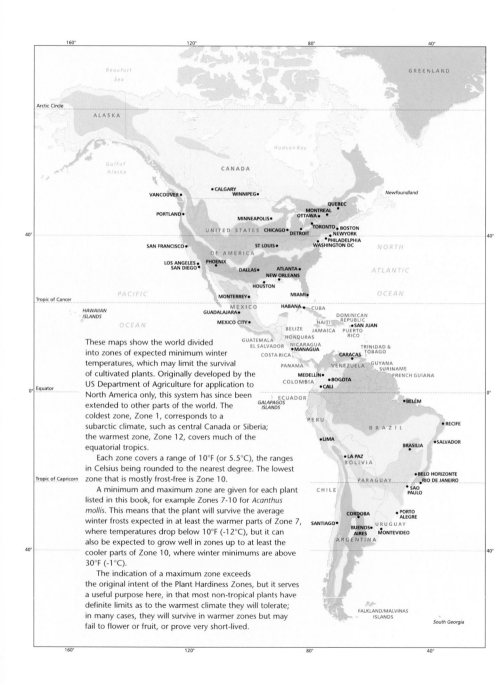

These maps show the world divided into zones of expected minimum winter temperatures, which may limit the survival of cultivated plants. Originally developed by the US Department of Agriculture for application to North America only, this system has since been extended to other parts of the world. The coldest zone, Zone 1, corresponds to a subarctic climate, such as central Canada or Siberia; the warmest zone, Zone 12, covers much of the equatorial tropics.

Each zone covers a range of 10°F (or 5.5°C), the ranges in Celsius being rounded to the nearest degree. The lowest zone that is mostly frost-free is Zone 10.

A minimum and maximum zone are given for each plant listed in this book, for example Zones 7-10 for *Acanthus mollis*. This means that the plant will survive the average winter frosts expected in at least the warmer parts of Zone 7, where temperatures drop below 10°F (-12°C), but it can also be expected to grow well in zones up to at least the cooler parts of Zone 10, where winter minimums are above 30°F (-1°C).

The indication of a maximum zone exceeds the original intent of the Plant Hardiness Zones, but it serves a useful purpose here, in that most non-tropical plants have definite limits as to the warmest climate they will tolerate; in many cases, they will survive in warmer zones but may fail to flower or fruit, or prove very short-lived.

INDEX